MOTO RUM
The complete sto

CW01095612

MOTO RUMI
The complete story

Riccardo Crippa

GIORGIO NADA EDITORE

Giorgio Nada Editore

Editorial Coordination
Luciano Greggio

Editing
Diana Calarco

Layout
Elena Fiori

Cover design
Marco Delise

Photographs by
Archivio Registro Storico Rumi
Giorgio Boschetti

English translation
Neil Frazer Davenport

© 2005 Giorgio Nada Editore, Vimodrone (MI) Italy

Giorgio Nada Editore s.r.l.
Via Claudio Treves, 15/17
I – 20090 VIMODRONE - MI
Tel. +39 02 27301126
Fax +39 02 27301454
E-mail: info@giorgionadaeditore.it
www.giorgionadaeditore.it

*The catalogue of
Giorgio Nada Editore
publications is
available on request
at the above address.*

Moto Rumi - The complete story
ISBN: 88-7911-364-X

Thanks:

The author and publisher wish to thank all of those who
have helped with material, documents, clarification and
advice during the creation of this book. They would
especially like to thank Franco Lavetti and Achille and
Oscar Rumi, whose co-operation has been as invaluable as
it has indispensable to the project. And finally, thanks also
go to Brizio Pignacca, who has contributed substantially to
the wording of the text.

CONTENTS

THE STORY OF A GREAT LITTLE MARQUE   8

RUMI TECHNOLOGY   24
The engine   24
The frame   32
The expansion chambers   40

RUMI PRODUCTION   42
Turismo (1950-1956)   42
Sport (1950-1958)   48
Competition SS 52 Gobbetto (1951-1955)   51
Scoiattolo (Squirrel) (1951-1957)   57
Regolarità (1952-1954) 1st and 2nd series   62
Bicarburatore (1953-1956)   67
G.T. - Granturismo (1953-1956)   71
Formichino (1954-1960)   73
Regolarità Sei Giorni (1955-1960)   79
Junior (1955-1959)   84
Diana (1955-1958)   88
Junior Gentleman (1959-1962)   92
125 Commercial three-wheeler (1950-1956)   96
Go-kart engines (1960-1966)   100
The "Rocket" engine   100
The "RS/C" engine   100
Amisa (1949) prototype   101

Grand Prix (1952) prototype   103
Bialbero (1953) prototype   107
V.T. - Valvole in testa (1954) prototype   110
Bicilindrica 4 tempi Rolla (1954) prototype   113
V1 Strada (1960) prototype   116
V1 Motoscooter (1960) prototype   122

RUMI PORTFOLIO   127

HONOUR ROLL 1950-1961   145

A SPORTING VOCATION   147
Rumi and competition   147
1950   150
1951   154
1952   159
1953   172
1954   188
1955   208
1956   225
1957   233
1958   238
1959   246
1960   249
1961   253

I have been asked to say my piece about this splendid publication, written by my friend and colleague, Riccardo Crippa. As I leafed through the proofs I became more and more convinced that the task of introducing the book was not going to prove a difficulty, but a pleasure.

Most people are aware of the deplorable dispersion of the Rumi archives in the years following the closure of the factory: this made it extremely difficult to provide irrefutably accurate information regarding either Rumi in general or the strictly technical aspects of the marque's motorcycle production.

But one thing is certain: technical experts and period bike enthusiasts were crying out for a reference book capable of solving the many problems faced by both professional restorers and fans alike.

The scrupulously accurate historic and technical information collated by the author should do much to bridge the gap. This volume will certainly become a source book of fundamental importance for those thinking of undertaking a restoration or for those who simply wish to learn a little more about the story of the marque and its contribution to motorcycle engineering. The second section of the book is made up of the Roll of Honour, a year by year account of Rumi's career in the world of competition and an essential adjunct to a work that traces the evolution of this extraordinary marque. An inconfutably accurate source of information, this section is far more than a mere list of results, but a sporting history in its own right from whose pages emerge the heroic and unselfish figures of the great riders of the past, the real protagonists of the "Rumi legend".

It ought to be said that the particular commitment and painstaking care that the author has brought to the task of recovering an endangered piece of our cultural history springs from a spirit of pure affection for this subject. When leafing through these pages, rich with splendid and rigorously authentic illustrations that well reflect the atmosphere of those years, the reader gains the impression – and this is what really counts – that he too is a part of the magnificent adventure as it gradually unfolds.

I have recently read Riccardo Crippa's history of the motorcycles built by my father Donnino Rumi in the Fifties. In the first place I ought to express the sense of sheer wonder I felt when faced with the wealth of details, information, and beautiful photographs that have been marshalled to form this exceptional book. I am also extremely happy that it was someone from my home town who took the trouble to seek out, analyse, select, and compile the multivarious pages of Rumi's sporting and technical history, a time-consuming task that must have required enormous patience and enthusiasm since the marque undoubtedly made an important contribution in terms of both styling and sporting success in those years.

As I worked alongside my father Donnino Rumi, I have first hand experience, right from the creation of the first bike, of those difficult but extraordinary years and I have therefore nothing but praise for this important piece of research. This is a handsome and comprehensive work that will certainly become a benchmark for all those who lived through that period, as well as for those who now want to know more about the development of these bikes, which were designed – especially as far as the cycle parts were concerned – by that man of no mean ability who was my father.

This volume is a form of well deserved recognition that should do much to prevent people from forgetting what was a unique experience both for myself and for all those who love these motorcycles.

Now, in 1992, forty years on, the passion we all shared for the roar of the Rumi twins has come alive once more, thanks to the author of this book and to all those who never forgot.

Finally, it is also thanks to these people that the memory of my father remains green; a man who never failed to appreciate what was new and beautiful, he did not always receive the recognition he deserved.

Benito Battilani
Chairman of the National Technical Commission
for Motorcycles ASI

Achille Rumi

THE STORY
OF A GREAT LITTLE MARQUE

The Rumi phenomenon and the company's entrance into the field of motorized transport coincided with a well defined period in Italian history. As the Forties drew to a close, Italy's primary concerns were reconstruction, transforming a predominantly agricultural economy to an industrial one, and dealing with new patterns of supply and demand at all social levels that were expected to follow.

After long years of tightened bells and sacrifice Italians had begun to rediscover a taste for prosperity. They longed not only for stable jobs that would allow them to live decently, but also for their own means of motorized transport, preferably something that was not too costly to run. In the field of two-wheeled transport the big names of the pre-war era made their reappearance. These firms were based mainly in Lombardy and were all involved in designing and producing honest to goodness utility motorcycles. Other companies, such as MV Agusta, Innocenti, and Ducati, were struggling to convert their production capacity, their human resources, and their available plant to a sector that would allow them to compensate for, at least in part, the drastic reduction in demand caused by the almost total cancellation of military contracts. So much for the prevailing industrial climate when the Rumi company was established.

In 1948, Rumi – then known as Fonderie Officine Srl, with its factory at number 225 in Bergamo's via Moroni and its head office in Milan – was at the peak of its industrial expansion with the works occupying a vast site on an industrial estate just outside Bergamo. The contemporary press described its modern premises, comprehensively equipped with modern industrial tooling and covering an area of over 20,000 square metres, as being of the "American" type.

Thanks to considerable experience gained through wartime contracts with the Navy and the state railway, Rumi had already established a reputation as an avant-garde engineering company as well as a bronze and aluminium foundry working on its own account and for third parties.

The easiest way for Rumi to reconvert to peacetime production would have been to engage in the construction of machinery for pasta factories and wooden mills – carding and combining machines and gill boxes – as export openings for this type of machinery did exist, but such a course would have been heavily penalized by the political obstructionism imposed in this area by the allied authorities who, at that time, exerted a strong influence over Italian business. The owner of the firm, Donnino Rumi, soon realized that an immediate diversification programme was required. He was also quick to realize the importance, given the requirements of industrial reconversion and the changing patterns of consumption of the immediate post-war period, oh the transport sector. Public transport was virtually inexistent and its development was left to the skills and initiative of individual entrepreneurs.

Donnino Rumi was born in 1906 in Bergamo and by the time he was twelve he was already working as an apprentice in his father Achille's foundry (established in 1914), which specialized in the production of bronze castings. At the same time he attended Bergamo's Carrera Academy. By 1926, at twenty years of age, he was actively involved in the thriving foundry where he worked hard to expand its potential. In just a few years Donnino's full and enthusiastic participation in the company's activities led to the transformation of the family firm into a solid business with a diversified

production capability. By the beginning of 1939 Rumi employed 100 persons and its production volume had already reached notable levels.

As was the case with numerous other workshops in Northern Italy during the war, the Germans had installed their own administrator responsible for overseeing munitions production. Donnino preferred to go into hiding rather than collaborate with the Germans and he joined a group of partisans operating in the Bergamo region. He was captured and imprisoned in 1943 and liberated in 1945. In that same year he resumed control of the Rumi works in the joint role of general manager and sole administrator.

Confident in his own technical abilities and in the experience and proven skills of the six hundred or so employees who worked for him, Rumi decided to begin producing small capacity, economical motorcycles. As far as the well established Bergamo firm was concerned this was a step into quite an unknown territory. Having chosen the direction that the company was to follow, Donnino Rumi was faced

Left, Donnino Rumi in 1952, and below, a view of the Rumi Factory dated the same year. The modern building in the foreground housed the administrative offices and the experimental division.

La **VOLPE**
è la macchina per tutti

La macchina per tutti
è la **VOLPE**

A drawing of the "Volpe" microcar, powered by a little two stroke twin cylinder engine specially designed by Pietro Vassena. No more than four of five demonstration units were produced, the sole aim being to encourage orders, but these never materialized. The "Volpe" was involved in a famous fraud case in the late Forties.

with a major problem: how to come up with a brand new design for the project. His choice of designer was an extremely good, if admittedly predictable one, since Pietro Vassena – a great motorboat designer considered by some to be an authentic genius in his field – was a long standing friend and client of Rumi. Vassena, who lived in nearby Lecco, felt quite at home at Bergamo. Whilst he was primarily a boat designer, he had never spurned the opportunity to design two- or four-wheeled motor vehicles. As early as 1926 he had designed and constructed a motorized bicycle fitted with a two-stroke horizontal single-cylinder engine which proved reasonably successful. Just for the record we should also point out that some years later, in 1953, Vassena also designed the revolutionary Automotoscooter 200 for the noted Carniti motorboat firm.

The collaboration between these two gifted men, both blessed with great imagination and devoid of the blinkered attitudes that were so common in the traditional motorcycle industry, proved decidedly fruitful. As it happened, Vassena had a design for a small 125 cm³ engine suitable for powering the Rumi motorcycle all ready and waiting. In 1946 he had designed and produced a few engines for the "Volpe" microcar, which was at the centre of a famous swindle. Fortunately, the designs, for which he had never received any form of payment, still belonged to Vassena and he could use them as he saw fit.

Thus, after a lengthy period of research and testing, a new light motorcycle was born. The two-stroke flat twin had a capacity of 125 cm³, the most popular size at the time for utility machines, and was mounted in an unusual tubular open cradle frame featuring some novel colour schemes. All these elements combined to achieve a reassuring degree of success right from the beginning.

The prototype was ready in the summer of 1949, and the engine in particular was widely considered to be something truly revolutionary. The two-stroke flat twin configuration was in complete contrast with the classic four-stroke vertical single, a design that dated back to the pioneering days of motorcycling history and one that had already found its way

into two- and four-stroke versions of 125 cm³ light motorcycle engines by 1949. The open duplex cradle frame was provisionally supplied for road testing by frame specialists A.M.I.S.A. of Milan.

Although the Rumi 125 was still not in mass production nor even on sale, it was presented to the public with its provisional frame in the December of 1949 at the Milan Cycle and Motorcycle Show. The public debut of the definitive version took place in March, 1950 at a Cycle and Motorcycle exhibition at the Donizzetti theatre in Bergamo, and immediately afterwards at the Milan Trade Fair in April. The motorcycle aroused considerable interest. Deliveries to customers began that month, whilst in the autumn, at the Milan Cycle and Motorcycle Show, the "Sport" model was presented on a somewhat grandiose stand. The newcomer met with success that went beyond all expectations.

Ing. Apice, in charge of machine tool design, was joined in the Rumi research and development office by Luigi Salmaggi, a top engineer who had worked for the Belgian firm Sarolea until 1938. He later went to Gilera at Arcore where he worked alongside the already famous engineer Piero Remor, recognized as the father of the blown "Rondine" four. Salmaggi was also responsible for the most celebrated 500 single built by Gilera, the "Saturno".

Salmaggi's particular genius lay in high performance engines and he recognized the enormous potential of the remarkable two-stroke twin. The designer's right-hand man was once again Orlando Ciceroni, nicknamed "Romanino", an expert engine tuner from the days of the "Rondine" in Rome. Together they created a topflight development department and concrete results, both on the current production side as well in competition, were not slow in coming.

The power output of the small twin rose from the 6 hp provided by the original unit to 7,5 hp, while production levels rose to thirty-two motorcycles per day. The specialized press gave the bike a lot of space but not all the comment was positive. Some praised the model, other damned it, but they all agreed that it went beyond anything that had so far been produced by the motorcycle industry, that the styling of the

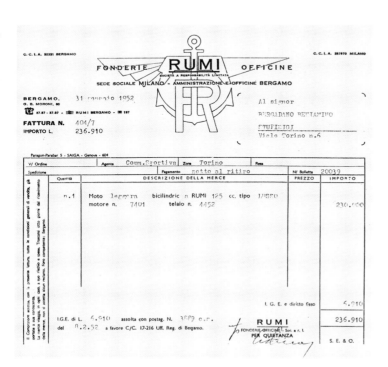

machine was impeccable and, lastly, that the exhaust pipes emitted a pleasant and unmistakeable note.

The racing division - which could count on excellent mechanics such as Natale Forcella, Luigi Vendemiello, Dino Ballerini, Vittorio Locatelli and Gianni Spreafico - carefully prepared the special bikes and harvested some gratifying results, particularly in long distance races and trial events. Rumi bravely decided to participate in the 26th International Six Day Trial, a notoriously tough event. To everyone's surprise Guglielmo Strada, a veteran trial specialist, brought home Rumi's first gold medal.

Rumi's great industrial and productive capacity was determined by the fact that all the components necessary for the assembly operations of its light motorcycles were actually produced in-house. The motorcycle division in particular was supplied with extremely sophisticated aluminium castings that still arouse admiration for their precision and high standards of workmanship. The workshops produced gears, con-rods and crankshafts, while the lightweight frame tubing was form and welded by specialized crafts-

men. Modern industrial practice, on the other hand, usually involves commissioning outside suppliers to produce the individual components while the parent company's factories handle assembly operations. This phenomenon was still unusual in the Fifties because companies specializing in the production of specific components were virtually inexistent and, therefore, only those firms capable of operating autonomously were able to produce machines with any reasonable guarantee of quality.

1953 proved to be the most fertile year of Rumi's motorcycle production career. Around 60 machines were coming off the production line every day and new models were being added to the catalogue. The "Scoiattolo" (Squirrel) scooter was flanked bye the "Gran Turismo", again powered by the flat twin 2-stroke engine, but with cylinder capacities of 175

and 200 cm³. In the meantime the racing department was preparing a 250 cm³, four-stroke grand prix twin engine designed by Luigi Salmaggi. It was Donnino Rumi's intention to enter the world of top level international competition, but unfortunately this remained a dream and the new twin was only ever seen in action during experimental testing at the Monza speedbowl in the spring of 1952.

An unusual assembly line was set up at the Bergamo works. The workers moved from place to place along the line in order to carry out successive individual assembly operations at the various stations. At that time the engine building department was equipped with a rather special "mobile workbench": the lower part of the crankcase casting was attached to a moving chain that ran around a bench, thus allowing each worker to carry out one assembly operation. When the circuit was completed the engine was fully assembled. Production levels rose still further, reaching seventy motorcycles per day. A vast sales and service network was organized both at home and abroad. As well as in Bergamo, branch offices were opened in some of Italy's most important cities including Rome, Milan, Bologna, Genoa and Verona. The sales outlets listed in an advertising pamphlet of the time comprised 25 dealers in Italy, 150 in Austria, 72 in France, 37 in England, 3 in Switzerland, 2 in Belgium and 21 in the United States of America. Furthermore, dealers were also present in numerous other countries: Malta, Holland, Norway, Portugal, Sweden, French Africa, Algeria, Morocco, Argentina, Chile, the Gold Coast, Indochina, Libya, Madagascar, Mexico, Senegal, South Africa, Uruguay, Paraguay, Tunisia, the Belgian Congo and Japan. An impressive network indeed, and one that was established in less than two years.

Donnino was the indefatigable and enthusiastic creative force behind all that went on in the Bergamo firm. His artis-

The 1953 Geneva Motor Show: moving from the left foreground towards the rear, two "Squirrels" - one with a sidecar - a "Sport", a "Turismo", and a "Gran Turismo" 200; right, the "Bicarburatore".

13

Above, the Rumi subsidiary in Bergamo's piazza della Libertà. Right, Rumi was a well equipped electro-mechanical works with its own foundry and an efficient research and development division. Motorcycle production was aided by the use of a specific apparatus like the test bench shown in the photo.

14

A snapshot taken during the famous "Valli Berga-masche" event: Donnino Rumi, with his wife Adriana, cheers on Guglielmo Strada from the roadside.

Right, the Rumi price
list. Note the "Compe-
tizione" version, alias the
"Gobbetto", was avail-
able with lights for long
distance events. Right,
the "Formichino" was in-
troduced, in typical Fi-
fites' style, at the 1955
Vienna Show. On the
facing page, Gianni Zon-
ca and Silvano Forcella,
seated on his Junior Ear-
les, in front of the Bergamo office in 1955.

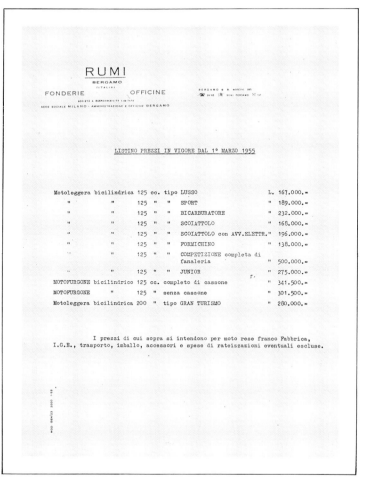

tic talent was confirmed by the original, but never gaudy colour
schemes, by the design of the fairings and the frames, model-
ling and remodelling them until he was completely satisfied.
His motorcycles not only had to be efficient but also attractive.
Even today certain models still have a thoroughly modern air.
Donnino Rumi was also ahead oh his times in terms of his
concern for ecology, a notion that was virtually unknown to
the general public at that time, but one which he had made
an integral part of his own personal philosophy. It was no
mere whim that led to the inclusion of the following message in the handbooks supplied with his motorcycles:
" *The Rumi motorcycle company appeals to its customers'*
sense of civic duty in asking them to do all they can to ensure
that their engines run quietly. "
The message goes on to say:
"*Precise regulations have been established at all service stations*
to ensure that no services, free or otherwise, is given to those
owners of Rumi motorcycles who have deliberately altered the
exhaust silencers or removed the glass fibre from the same. "

On the roof of the factory directly communicating with his
office, Donnino Rumi had a studio built with a large picture
window that looked out over the architectural marvels of
upper Bergamo. Here he was able to cultivate his favourite
hobby of painting. It is interesting to note in the monograph
dedicated to his paintings, published by Editrice Bolis on be-
half of his son Achille, just how many of his works of that
period are views of Bergamo's splendid High Town.
To return to more specific company matters, in the September
of 1953 the head designer, Ing. Salmaggi, was replaced by Ing.
Bruno Guidorossi. The latter came from the Milan firm MAS
for which he had designed the "Stella Alpina" (1947), a 122
cm³, four-stroke single with forced air cooling, and the "Zenit"
(1951), a robust 175 cm³, four-stroke, ohv unit. Later,
Guidorossi was joined in the design department by Ing. Nopler.
As far as diversification of production is concerned, in 1954
the Rumi catalogue, which was already notable for the
quantity and quality of the machines available, was enlarged with the introduction of new models and came to

16

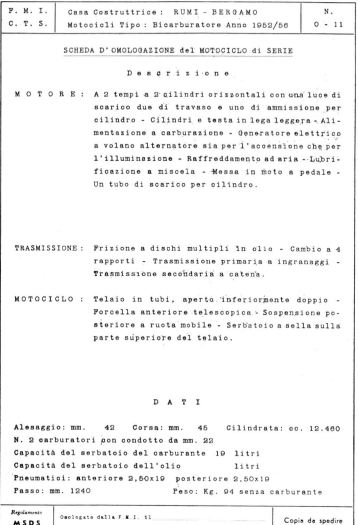

| F. M. I. | Casa Costruttrice : RUMI - BERGAMO | N. |
| C. T. S. | Motocicli Tipo : Bicarburatore Anno 1952/56 | O - 11 |

SCHEDA D'OMOLOGAZIONE del MOTOCICLO di SERIE

Descrizione

MOTORE : A 2 tempi a 2 cilindri orizzontali con una luce di scarico due di travaso e uno di ammissione per cilindro - Cilindri e testa in lega leggera - Alimentazione a carburazione - Generatore elettrico a volano alternatore sia per l'accensione che per l'illuminazione - Raffreddamento ad aria - Lubrificazione a miscela - Messa in moto a pedale - Un tubo di scarico per cilindro.

TRASMISSIONE : Frizione a dischi multipli in olio - Cambio a 4 rapporti - Trasmissione primaria a ingranaggi - Trasmissione secondaria a catena.

MOTOCICLO : Telaio in tubi, aperto inferiormente doppio - Forcella anteriore telescopica - Sospensione posteriore a ruota mobile - Serbatoio a sella sulla parte superiore del telaio.

DATI

Alesaggio: mm. 42   Corsa: mm. 45   Cilindrata: cc. 12.460
N. 2 carburatori con condotto da mm. 22
Capacità del serbatoio del carburante 19 litri
Capacità del serbatoio dell'olio   litri
Pneumatici: anteriore 2,50x19 posteriore 2,50x19
Passo: mm. 1240   Peso: Kg. 94 senza carburante

| Regolamento **M S D S** 1956 | Omologato dalla F.M.I. il .... Il Direttore Generale F M I .... | Copia da spedire al Costruttore |

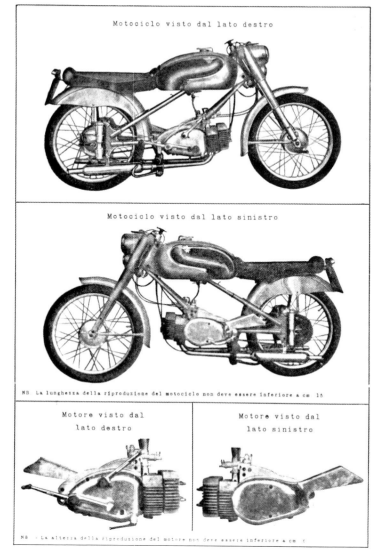

Motociclo visto dal lato destro

Motociclo visto dal lato sinistro

NB - La lunghezza della riproduzione del motociclo non deve essere inferiore a cm 15

| Motore visto dal lato destro | Motore visto dal lato sinistro |

NB - La altezza della riproduzione del motore non deve essere inferiore a cm 6

comprise the following: the 125 "Turismo" and "Sport", the "Scoiattolo" scooter (also available with an electric starter), the 175 and 200 cm³ versions of the "Gran Turismo", the new "Formichino" scooter which many consider to be Rumi's masterpiece, and the 175 VT four-stroke vertical single - a machine which, unfortunately, never got beyond the prototype stage. Lastly there were the sporting or racing models: the SS 52 "Gobbetto" racer, and a brand new trials machine whose frame and swinging arm suspension had been specially devised by Guidorossi.

At the end of that year Rumi signed a deal with the Belgian company Sarolea for the production of the "Formichino" under licence. In Belgium the scooter was rebaptized the "Dyninn" and was presented at the Brussels Show in January, 1955. The event was a source of great pride and encouragement for the Bergamo firm as Sarolea was an extremely well known motorcycle manufacturer founded before the turn of the century. Until then, Sarolea's model range had lacked a scooter, a vehicle which - thanks to the Vespa and the Lambretta - had by then conquered a considerable share of the two-wheeled market in Europe and farther afield. That the Belgian firm had opted for the "Formichino" was further confirmation of the technical and aesthetic qualities of the Rumi product. Exports, in particular to Latin America countries, grew to substantial levels. The European market, however, was by no mean any less important: in the spring a batch of 120 light motorcycles was sent to Sweden, and 140 machines went to Switzerland.

SCHEDA D'OMOLOGAZIONE del MOTOCICLO di SERIE

D e s c r i z i o n e

M O T O R E : A due tempi a 2 cilindri orizzontali con 1 scarico, 2 luci travaso e una spirazione per cilindro - cilindro e testa in lega leggera - Alimentazione a carburazione - Accensione e Generatore elettrico a volano alternatore - Raffreddamento ad aria - Lubrificazione a miscela - messa in Moto a pedale   un tubo di scarico per cilindro

TRASMISSIONE : Frizione a dischi multipli in olio
Cambio di velocità a 4 rapporti
Trasmissione primaria a ingranaggi
Trasmissione secondaria a catena

M O T O C I C L O : Telaio in tubi aperto
Sospensione anteriore telescopica
Sospensione posteriore a braccio oscillante
Serbatoio carburante a sella

D A T I

Alesaggio : mm.   42   Corsa :   mm.   45   Cilindrata : cc.   124.60

N. 2 carburatori con condotto da mm. 16.5

Capacità del serbatoio del carburante 18 litri

Capacità del serbatoio dell'olio   - - - litri

Pneumatici : anteriore 2.50 x 19   posteriore 2.50 x 19

Passo : mm. 1250   Peso : Kg. 77

Regolamento
MSDS
1956

Omologato dalla F. M. I. il 29 Marzo 1957

Il Direttore Generale F. M. I. Dr. Ing. G. Bariona

Motociclo visto dal lato destro

Motociclo visto dal lato sinistro

N.B. - La lunghezza della riproduzione del motociclo non deve essere inferiore a cm. 15

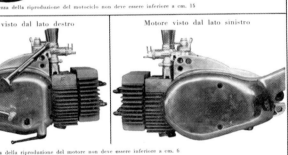

Motore visto dal lato destro   Motore visto dal lato sinistro

N.B. - La altezza della riproduzione del motore non deve essere inferiore a cm. 6

The original IMF homologation papers (for the year 1957) which the Rumi "Junior" required in order to race in Sport class competition. In 1959 the same "Junior" model and the "Bicarburatore" were homologated afresh, even though the only variant regarded the inlet manifold, which became 18 mm for the "Junior" and 22 mm for the "Bicarburatore", as required by changes in the IMF rule book.

1955 was also the year in which the "Junior" 125 was presented. This was undoubtedly the best-loved and most sought-after bike by the youngsters of the time since it represented a rare chance for would-be racers to get a foot in the door of the magical world of motorcycles competition. In exchange for a relatively modest outlay young lads could get hold of a reliable machine with sparkling performance and road burning acceleration. Running through the "Junior's" roll of honour many years later reveals that it enjoyed notable success both in short circuit races and in long distance events. The "Junior" model featured a brand new frame and suspension was fitted with aluminium cylinders with chromed barrels, a feature usually reserved for Grand Prix machines at that time. The engine could pump out 9 hp at 8000 rpm.

Although sales volumes remained at acceptable levels, the following year saw the Fonderie Officine Rumi come up against the first signs of trouble. The problems most probably arose as a result of liquidity problems caused by high production levels inadequately supported by the commercial structure. The consequence of this was a surplus of unsold machines, which meant shutting down the lines for some months. This undoubtedly undermined Rumi's image as a prestigious avant-garde firm while its credibility was weakened as far as dealers were concerned. Many potential customers were lost.

It should be borne in mind that those years between 1953 and 1958 have been described as a "magical" period for the Italian motorcycle industry. The powerful Gilera firm of Ar-

Above, the Milan Trade Fair of April 1958. In the foreground, the pressed steel 150 cm³ "Formichino STEC"; behind, the "Sport" with the dualseat and the "Lusso"; left, the "Junior" with the Earles forks and bikini fairing. On the facing page, the prototype shop at the Rumi works.

core, the second largest Italia n manufacturer in terms of overall production, increased its total sales from around 10.000 units in 1951 to 21.500 in 1953. By 1958 this figure had fallen again to 18.500. Although a late arrival on the motorcycle manufacturing scene, Rumi had apparently sold as many as 21,600 machines by 1953, and so it is not unreasonable to suggest that it could have rivalled or even overtaken the giant Gilera firm had adequate financing been arranged. The production range remained unchanged in the following years if one excludes slight modifications made to the most popular models, the "Formichino", the "Junior" and the 125

"Turismo" and "Sport". Construction of the competition models was abandoned. A version of the "Formichino" was designed and produced with a pressed steel frame, a move intended to reduce production costs and to increase the machine's market share, especially abroad. Rumi possessed a wealth of experience in the export business and considerable resources were diverted in this direction. Unfortunately, after positive early results, quantities of motorcycles sent to South America were, for complex political reasons, never paid for, thus further aggravating the company's already precarious economic situation.

20

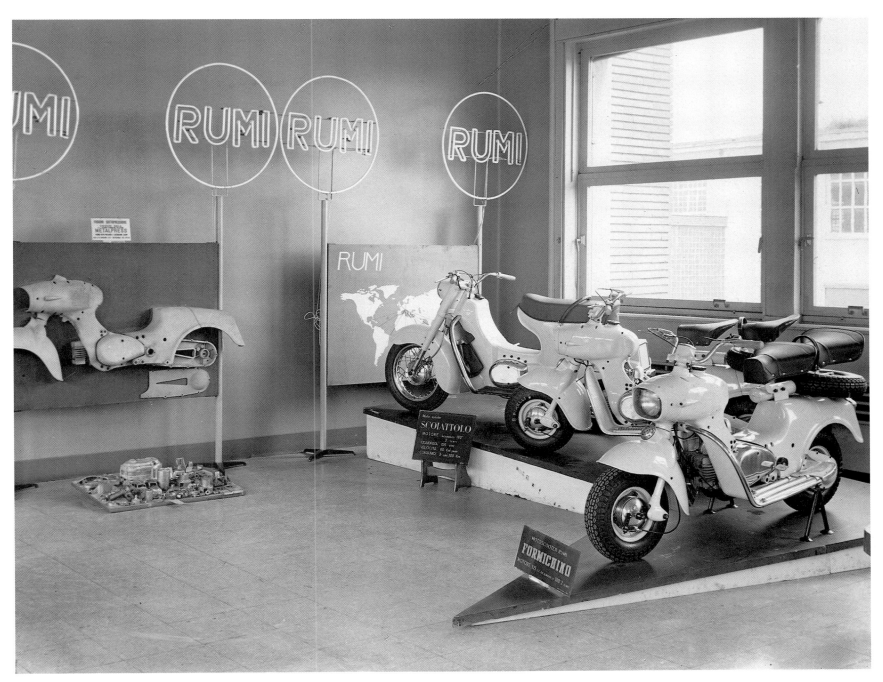

Right, the 1958 Saigon Motor Show. Below, the 1960 Milan Show; the new "V1" scooter is on the centre of the stand flanked on the right by 98 and 125 cm³ versions of the "Strada" and two versions of the classic "Formichino" and on the left by a "Strada" 125. On the facing page, another shot of the stand. From left to right, the new version of the "Junior Gentleman 125", the Rumi-Dogi go-kart by Italkart, the V1 engine and, finally, the 175 cm³ "Gentleman Corsa".

There was a surprise in store for those potential clients who flicked trough the 1961 Rumi catalogue. Alongside the well known models there was a revolutionary engine, a design worthy of the technical expertise that the firm had developed over a decade of motorcycle production. The unit in question was a longitudinal, four-stroke, 90° V-twin with cylinder capacities varying from 98 to 125 to 175 cm³. It was designed by Ing. Umberto Ottolenghi and was intended to power both motorcycles and scooters. The chassis of the scooter and the frame of the motorcycle were both innovatory in concept.

Although these models unfortunately remained at the prototype stage, they nevertheless bear eloquent testimony to the inventiveness of the Rumi company. After many vicissitudes the Rumi firm closed down for good in 1962.

After the company had ceased trading Donnino Rumi dedicated himself with his customary passion to what was his natural vocation, painting. He died at his birthplace, Bergamo, on the 17th of August, 1980.

RUMI TECHNOLOGY

THE ENGINE

Throughout the history of the Rumi motorcycle its strongest suit and the element that aroused the greatest interest was undoubtedly the engine. This was a unit that, as mentioned earlier, was the object of as much praise as criticism and today the debate remains open amongst enthusiasts and engineers: was it or was it not a great engine?

If I might be allowed to make a comment with regard to this issue, I would remind readers that the engine's detractors have constantly harped upon a certain fragility; on the other hand, its supporters have tended to emphasise the dynamism of its performance which was without doubt superior to that which could be achieved with any other road-going 125 cc unit.

It should also be added that on diverse occasions when it was subjected to extreme conditions, the engine successfully demonstrated its ability to cope with continuous high stress such as that imposed by long-distance racing. The Milan-Taranto race, for example, covered a distance of 1,400 kilometres, while the motorcycling Giro d'Italia covered almost 3,500 kilometres in stages.

The inventiveness of the engine's design provided its constructors with great satisfaction, as much from the point of view of mass production as that of its thermal efficiency (power output rose from the 6hp of the early model to the 9hp of the final examples). The crankcase was composed of two cast-aluminium half-shells assembled horizontally so as to facilitate both the production of the castings themselves and the subsequent assembly. The two small cylinders - that in the case of the early examples were in cast-iron and later in cast-aluminium - were equipped with special cooling fins arranged on two planes at right-angles to one-another and were fixed to the crankcase via four simple but effective studs. The pistons were of course in aluminium, in two or three sections, and fitted with a special system of dual scavenging deflectors patented by Rumi. This scavenging system came in for constant criticism as it was considered to be inefficient compared with the more rational flat-crowned Schnurle system pistons that were already well known and widely adopted in the period.

The Rumi company was also ahead of its time in the use of expansion chambers in the exhaust system, and whilst the

Top left and right, views of the assembled engine. Bottom left, the engine during the final stages of assembly: still to be fitted, on this side, are the flywheel-magneto, the sprocket and the outer casing. Bottom right, a view of the left side of the "Scoiattolo" engine without the casing showing the flywheel magneto and the carburettor with filter. Note the upper drillings and the lower lugs for the attachment of the bodywork.

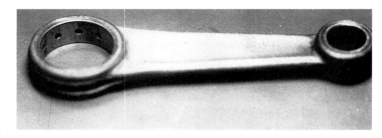

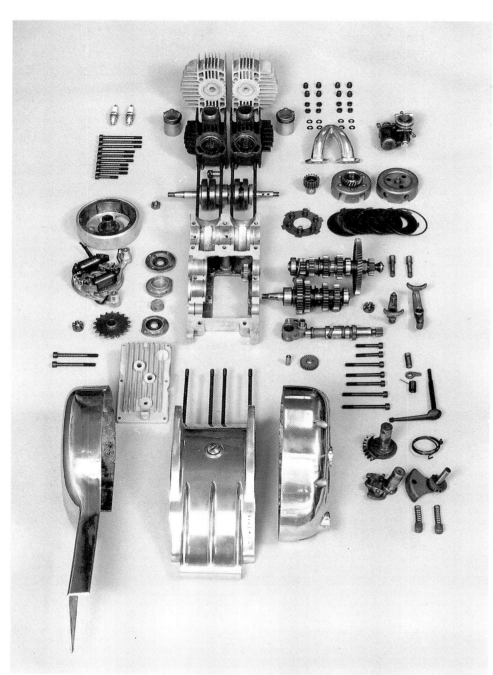

adoption of deflectors on the pistons did not exactly frustrate these experiments, it did overshadow them somewhat. Average pistons speeds could moreover reach 9.04 metres per second. The crankshaft, firmly located by three robust bearings, had the flywheel magneto keyed to one end with the helical-tooth primary transmission gear that transmitted power to the gearbox on the other. The gearbox itself was a constant mesh unit with straight-cut gears located in the crankcase. Initially it offered three speeds, but later a fourth ratio was adopted. The sprocket was therefore found on the left-hand side of the motorcycle. The transmission was set in an oil bath with the same lubricant being used for the crankshaft in a patented system clearly inspired by marine engine design practice. The cylinders and con-rods were lubricated by the petroil mixture.

The clutch, mounted on the right-hand side, was a multiple-plate unit, while the induction system, initially located in the crankcase, utilised one or two carburettors depending on the model, set vertically above the cylinders and equipped with elbowed intake tracts as used on the famous Moto Guzzi singles. Only the sports models were fitted with (generally two) horizontally mounted, twin-choke carburettors with straight intake manifolds. Ignition was via HT coil fed by the magneto that was located on the left of the crankcase and also acted as a flywheel. The ignition system might be considered as the machine's true Achilles' heel as electrical components of mediocre quality were used. Had leading specialist companies been commissioned to supply the magnetos, the coils and other electrical components then a slight increase in production costs and list prices would have been countered by improved results and a more reliable engine.

The entire range of Rumi production models, which offered differing specifications and levels of performance, was powered by the same basic engine, differentiated by marginal modifications to the gear ratios, the intake system and the cylinder types. It is by no means overstating the case to claim that the true potential of this little engine was never fully realized.

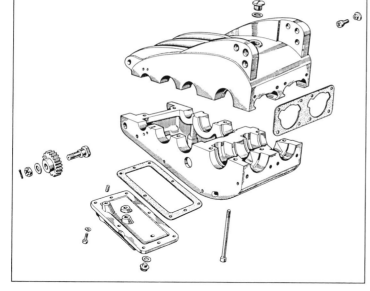
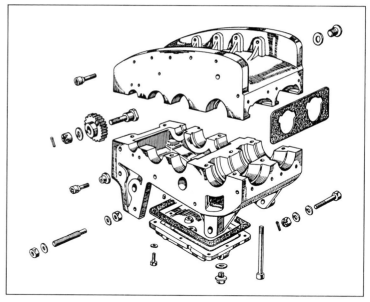

Left, the standard block for the 1950 "Turismo" and "Sport" models; right, the block used for the "Scoiattolo": the sole difference between the latter and the standard type consisted of the different attachment points for the frame. Below, the new block for the engine which, fitted for the first time in 1953 to the "Turismo Lusso", was subsequently used for all the sporting models. Note the widespread use of lightened castings and the cooling fins at the base of the cylinder.

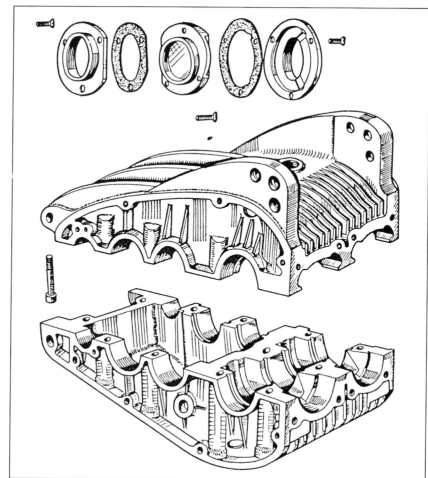

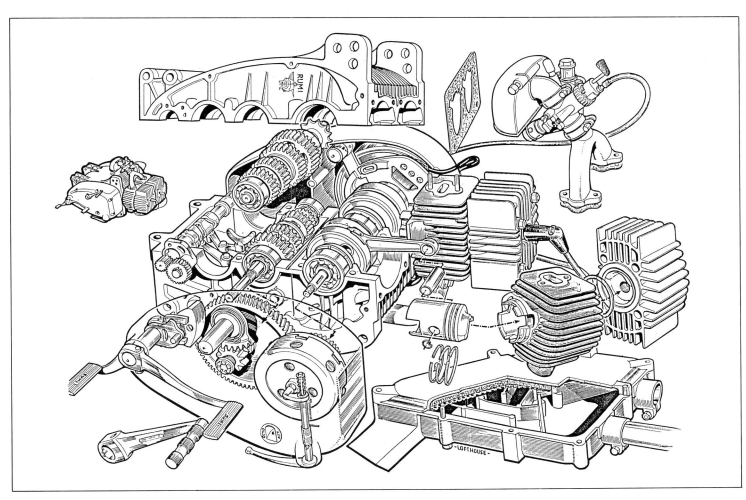

Left, an exploded drawing of the "Formichino" engine made in 1960 by the famous English draughtsman Lofthouse; note the small sketch of the recomposed engine on the left of the larger drawing. Below, the engine block: in this case too only the frame pickup points were non-standard. As it was produced in 1959, this engine was already equipped with the supplementary cooling fins.

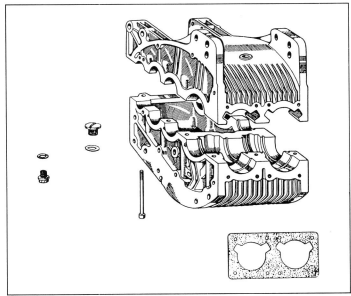

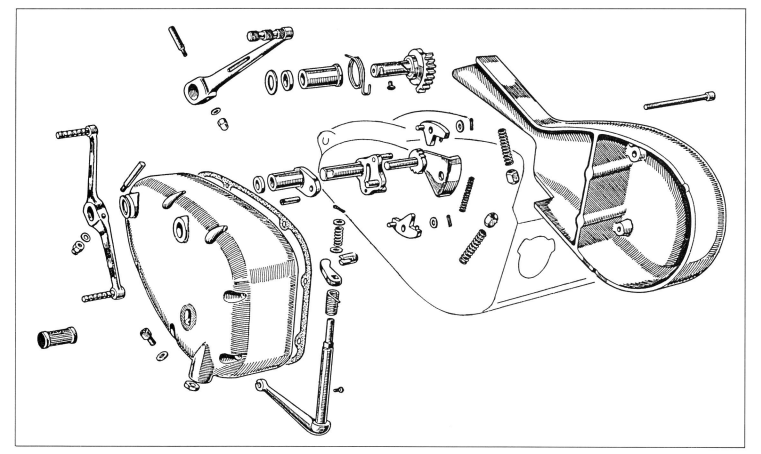

Right, the lateral casings, the levers and the preselector: these parts were interchangeable for all models. Below, the innards of the three-speed box fitted to "Turismo" models from 1950 to 1952, after which they went out of production.

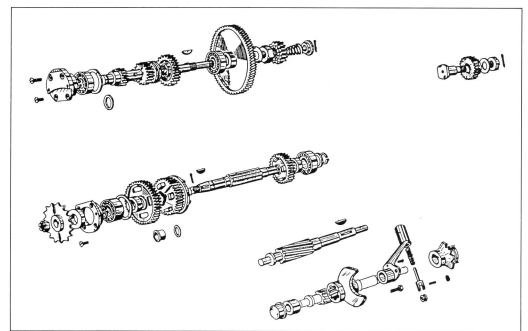

30

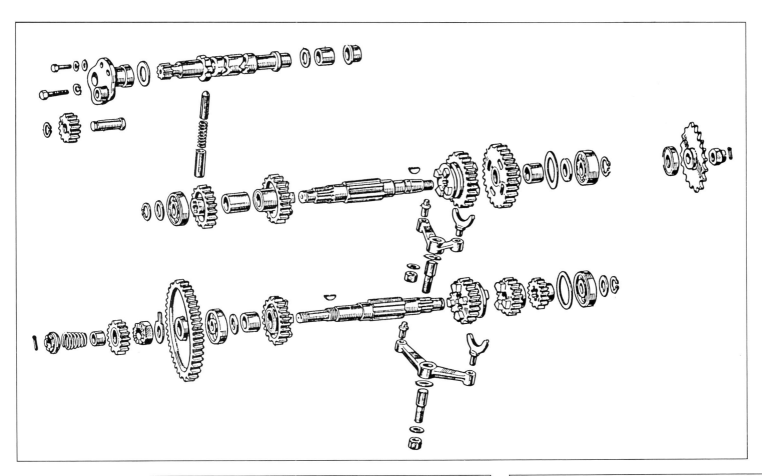

Left, the four-speed gearbox mounted in the "Sport" at the beginning of 1951, which, with different ratios, was later fitted to all models. Below left, the clutch, the crankshaft, the pistons, the cast iron cylinders and the aluminium heads with larger finning, which were adopted after 1953; below right, the particular fuel feed system on the "Bicarburatore" with the characteristic oval air filter that fed the twin carbs.

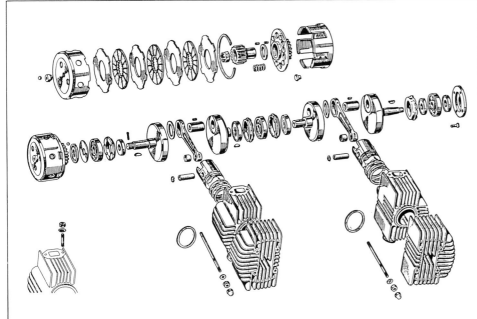

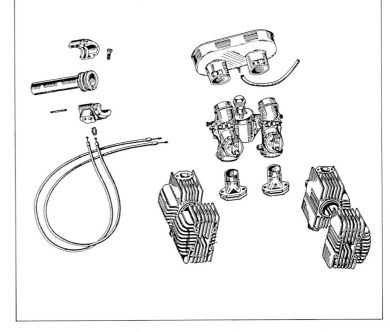

31

THE FRAME

The cradle frame was constructed in light steel tubing with the lower section open and linked to the engine at the top and the rear end of the crankcase creating in effect a kind of cantilevered engine architecture. In more detail, the frame was composed as follows:

- two tubes ran below the fuel tank, directly linking the steeringhead and the rear suspension;
- two further tubes welded to the lower end of the steeringhead were attached to the engine via two quadrilateral flanges;
- at the rear, two short tubes linked the engine to the rear fork; these tubes, connecting with the top tubes via a metal web, carried the sprung rear suspension.

The front suspension was also telescopic, with high-mounted guides and springs and was mounted in unit with the steeringhead via two large light alloy plates protected by a cowling that incorporated the headlight, the horn and the speedometer-odometer.

The rear suspension on the other hand was of the counter spring guided-wheel type, while the cantilevered saddle with a return spring under the fuel tank, was composed of a padded cast-aluminium shell upholstered in leather.

The motorcycle had a wheelbase of 1250 mm and the frame weighed 7.3 kg. During the course of its production life, it was never felt necessary to make any substantial changes to the main frame, while the telescopic fork and the rear suspension were modified and perfected.

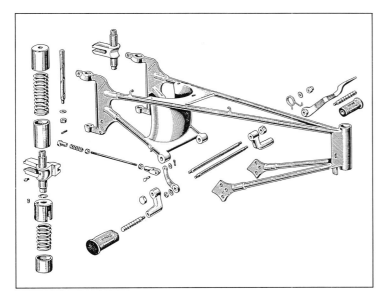

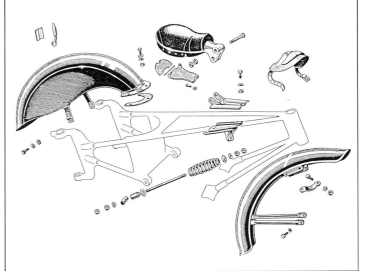

Top left, the frame, the beefed-up rear springing and the rear brake linkages. The design of the frame remained unchanged, except in the case of the "Bicarburatore", whose cradle had slightly wider front tubes anchored on the outside of the engine flanges in order to house the two carburettors. The same structure was adopted for the "Gobbetto", whose rear frame triangulation was also modified. Top right, the front and rear mudguards: note the system used to anchor the overhanging saddle to the two upper frame rails. Left, the large drawing shows the headlight cowling and the telescopic front forks with the top-mounted springs fitted to the "Turismo", "Sport" and "Scoiattolo" models until 1953.

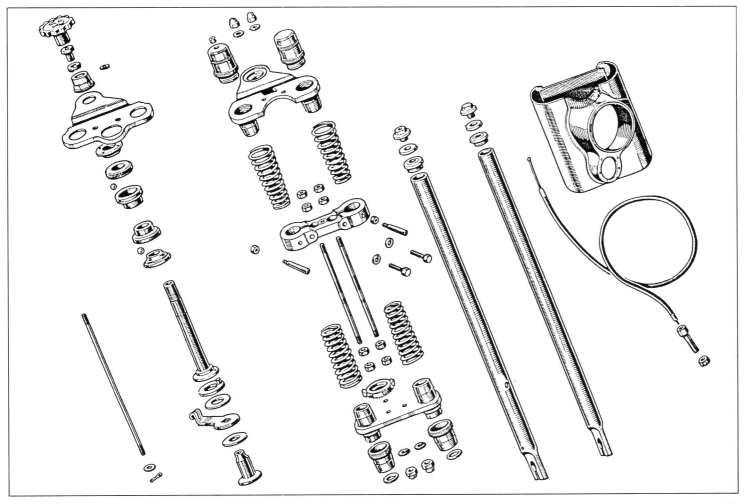

Right, the front mudguard and the new hydraulically damped telescopic fork was first fitted to the "Sport" in 1953 and subsequently to the entire range; the "Junior" mounted this fork with slightly shorter fork covers. Bottom left, the tank, exhaust pipes, and carburettors. The tilted carburettor on the left was fitted to the "Turismo", the vertical instrument (on the right) to the "Sport". The tanks varied according to models and types, while the stand - which also supported the exhausts - was later modified. Bottom right, the dualseat, the front mudguard and the fork covers of the "Turismo Lusso".

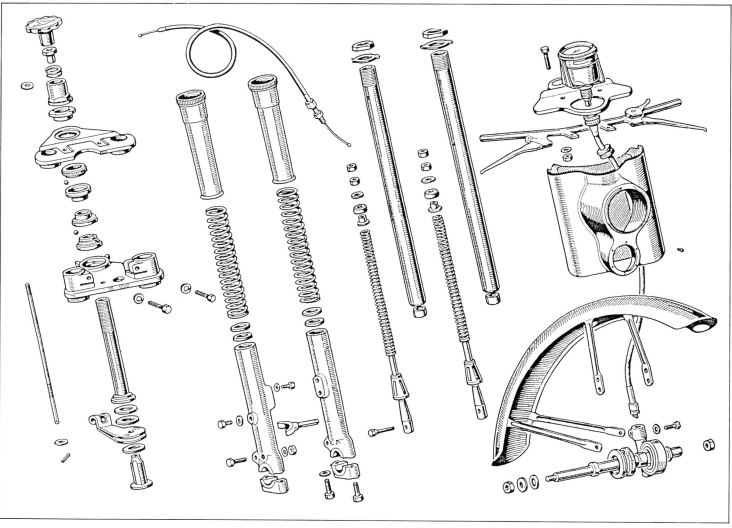

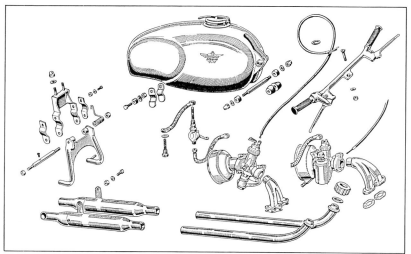

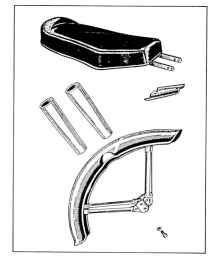

34

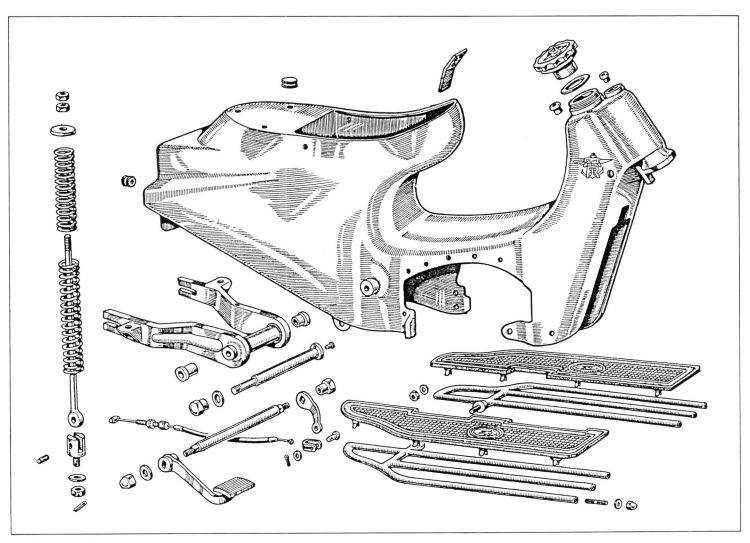

Left, the pressed steel bearing body, the running boards, and the rear springing of the "Scoiattolo"; in the type with the electric starter the batteries were housed in the spacious tool box beneath the saddle. Bottom left, further details of the "Scoiattolo" showing the saddle, the legshields and the front mudguard; bottom right, the handle bars, the exhaust pipes and the carburettor.

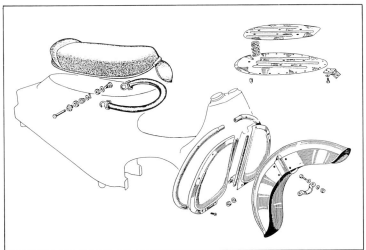

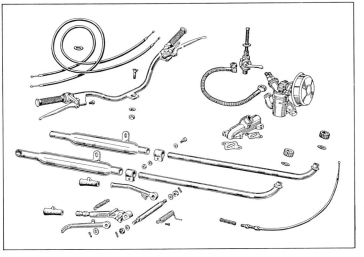

Right, the stressed body of the "Formichino": until 1955 the rear fairing was cast in one piece, but the introduction of new die-casting plant later made it more practical to split the casting in two (as shown in the drawing). Below, left, the cast aluminium monoarm rear suspension with the incorporated chainguard; springing was provided by a shock absorber made up of a series of rubber rings. Below, right, the leading link front fork built to replace the monoarm unit, considered too costly, fitted to the prototype in 1954.

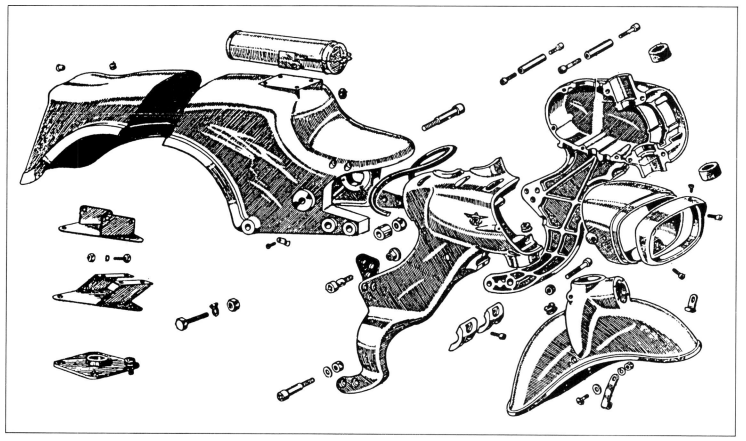

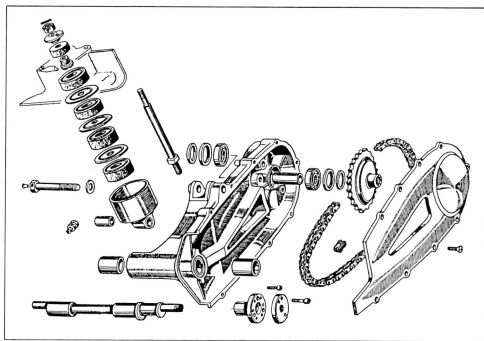

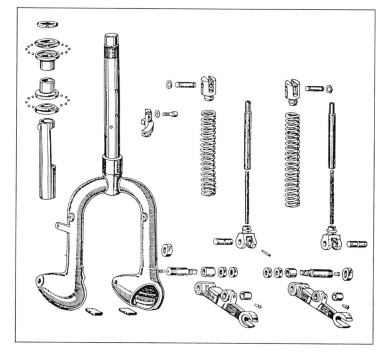

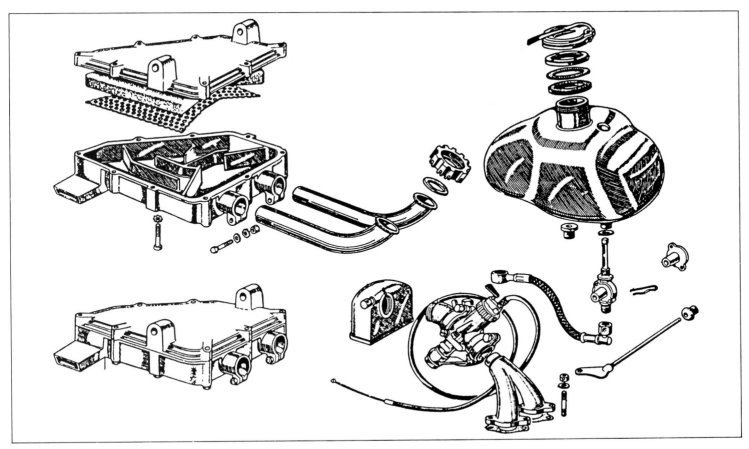

Another three drawings of the "Formichino". Left, the tank, the silencer with its internal "baffle", and the carburettor, protected by a downwards facing air filter. Below, left, the running boards and the legshields: note the two-piece die-cast saddle mountings held together with bolts; in the models built up to 1956 the mountings were integral with the bodywork. Below, right, the handle bars and the steering yoke plates: on the right of the drawing, the plates fitted until 1955; on the left, the type fitted thereafter, which could also house the odometer.

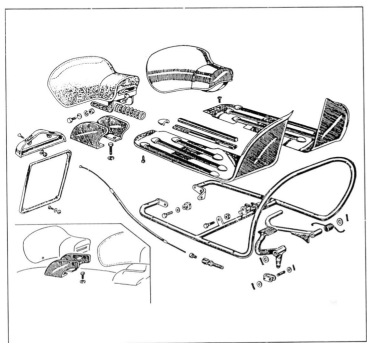

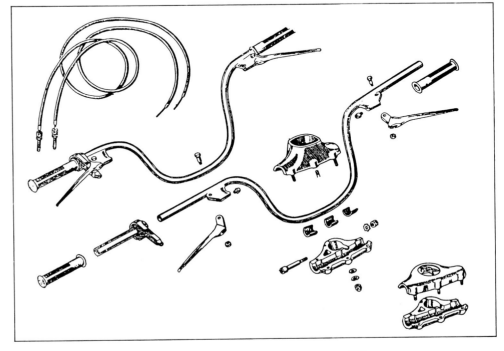

Right, the "Turismo Sport" electrics were also fitted to all successive models barring the competition bikes, which were equipped with an external magneto. The HT coil was later substituted by two separate coils, which were considered more reliable. Below, the electrics of the "Scoiattolo": note the HT coil with the two outlets for the spark plugs.

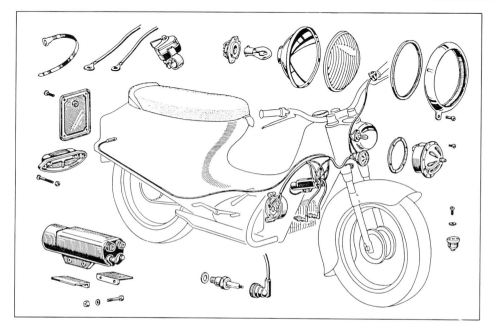

38

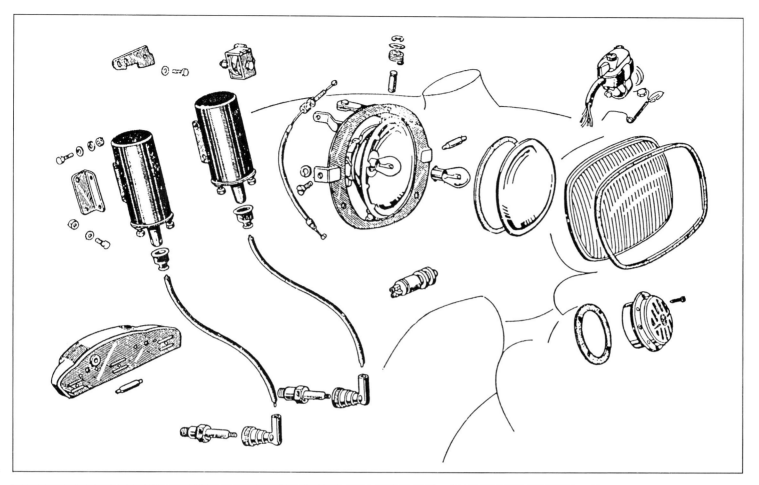

Left, the electrical system of the "Formichino" showing the separate HT coils. Note the swivelling headlight controlled by a cord at the steering head. Below, left, all the Rumi strokers used this type of magneto, naturally with a twin contact, which also doubled as a flywheel. Bottom right, this electric starter (or dynamotor) complete with a 6 Volt battery was fitted to the "Scoiattolo" after 1953 in exchange for a small extra charge.

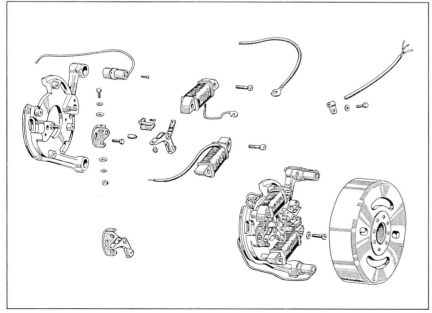

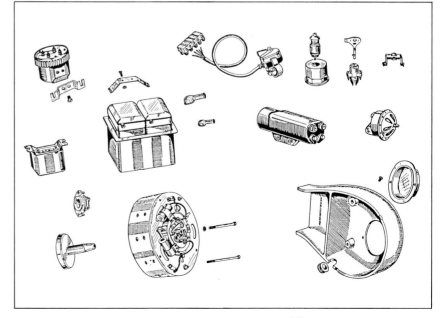

THE EXPANSION CHAMBERS

One of the features on which the Rumi engineers focussed their attention once the company had gained experience in the field of two-stroke engines was the shape and dimensions of the exhaust pipes. It had, in fact, been noted that the configuration of the exhaust system could have a beneficial effect on engine efficiency. Drawing on earlier experiments in the field conducted by Garelli in the 1920s, the engineer Guidorossi was able to verify the motives for which the shape of the exhaust had a certain influence on the performance of the power unit.

He soon realised that the periodic variations in exhaust gas pressure might, if appropriately channelled in specially shaped ducts, favour the extraction of residual gases in the combustion chamber, a defect that was typical of two-stroke engines. Moving on to practical test-bench experimentation, Rumi eventually identified an unusual expansion chamber with two opposed cones as the optimum form for an exhaust system that would significantly improve the efficiency of the engine, especially at low revs. This type of exhaust had been adopted in 1925 on the two-stroke, twin-cylinder Garelli 350.

The new exhaust was disguised by a section of cylindrical tubing, in part due to the aesthetic reservations expressed by Donnino Rumi with regard to a dual-cone system, and in part to legitimate concerns over industrial privacy. The expansion chambers, as we believe it is right to call them even though the term was unknown at the time, were fitted for the first time to two examples of the Junior entered for the 1955 Motorcycling Giro d'Italia and which provided highly satisfactory results.

Guidorossi, the Rumi engineer, recalls that at the end of a race, Angelo Copeta, an MV Agusta rider in the 125 cc Grand Prix category, asked him what kind of devilry he had introduced to Zonca's Rumi as it had become uncatchable out of corners. The merit was, of course due to the expansion chambers.

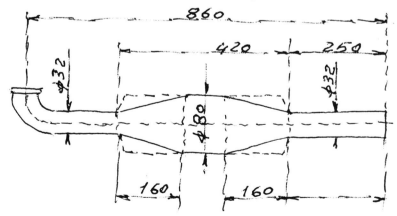

Tubo scarico motore Rumi bicilindrico bicarburatore 125 cm^3 - competizione.

860
420 250
ø32 ø80 ø32
160 160

Tubo studiato per lo sfruttamento della variazione periodica della pressione dei gas discarico.

1955 -

40

RUMI PRODUCTION

This second version of the "Turismo", complete with new colour schemes and partially chromed tank, was introduced in the November of 1950. Both the cycle parts and the mechanicals had been improved.

"TURISMO" (1950-1956)

The "Turismo" model was the first bike to come off the Rumi production line. It was introduced at the Milan Trade Fair in April 1950 after having made its debut at a Cycle and Motorcycle Show held in Bergamo one month before. The machines began to be delivered to customers in April and in the October of the same year the range of available colour schemes was modified: for example the fuel tank, which previously was chromed, was painted the same colour as the frame. At the end of November a new model was presented that featured notable improvements to both engine performance - maximum engine speed was increased to 5400 rpm - and the cycle parts. The front forks, which were originally connected with cast bronze yokes, were lightened and improved with the fitting of a fourth internal spring. The rear dampers were, in turn, improved and sheathed in chromed cylindrical sleeves. The "Turismo" model was joined by the "Turismo Lusso" in the 1953 catalogue. A new engine type was fitted featuring ample finning below the crankcase to improve cooling, high turbulence light alloy cylinder heads with oval combustion chambers, pistons fitted with a special deflector and a four-speed gearbox.

A hydraulically damped telescopic front fork with sleeves on the fork stanchions and four internal springs took care of the front suspension and steering. The mudguard had four struts and the larger capacity fuel tank was of a different shape. It was also possible to specify a dualseat for riding two-up.

In 1955 the teledraulic front fork was further improved with the adoption of the classic cast aluminium headlamp cowling, and the diameter of the rear dampers was also increased.

Production ceased in 1956.

Above, the "Turismo" introduced in November 1950; note the silencers, later modified, and the subframe for the pillion pad. Left, the "Turismo" was also available with a sidecar (optional) made in cast aluminium by Durapid of Rome.

43

125 CM³ "TURISMO" (1950-1956)

ENGINE	*two-stroke, parallel flat twin*
DISPLACEMENT	*124.68 cm³*
BORE AND STROKE	*42 x 45 mm*
COMPRESSION RATIO	*6.6:1*
MAXIMUM RPM	*4,800 rpm*
MAXIMUM POWER	*6 hp (3 fiscal hp in Italy)*
CYLINDER HEADS AND BARRELS	*separate cast iron barrels; heads first in iron, then in aluminium*
CARBURETTOR	*Dell'Orto UA 15 S with dual inlet manifold*
CARBURETTOR DATA	*choke tube 15, coupling M23, valve 55, jet 262, tapered needle C7, 3rd notch, max. jet 60, min. jet 45, toggle 48, float 7.5, inclined float chamber, air intake with filter*
IGNITION	*flywheel magneto with two contact breakers, two sparks per cycle, 6 V 30 W*
CLUTCH	*wet multiplate*
GEARBOX	*unit construction 3-4-speed in constant mesh*
GEAR RATIOS	*3 speeds: 1st 21.7, 2nd 12.8, 3rd 8.0* *4 speeds: 1st 26.4, 2nd 16.0, 3rd 10.8, 4th 8.5;*
DRIVE	*geared primary, chain secondary*
FRAME	*open duplex cradle*
WHEELBASE	*1250 mm*
FRONT SUSPENSION	*telescopic fork with springs in the upper part*
REAR SUSPENSION	*return springs covered with rubber gaiters*

WHEELS	*36 tangential wire spokes laced onto iron or aluminium rims*
TYRES	*from 2.50 x 18" - front: ribbed; rear: grooved*
BRAKES	*140 mm aluminium expanding shoe brakes*
ELECTRICAL SYSTEM	*Nassetti magneto, CEV headlight, CEV rear light*
INSTRUMENTATION	*VDO speedometer reading from 1-100 km/h*
RIDING POSITION	*cantilever saddle/dualseat*

Left, the "Turismo": the tank, chromed at first, was painted the same colour as the frame in October 1951. On the facing page, the first version of the "Turismo" in its sombre black livery.

45

Left, the 1955 "Lusso": neither the legshields nor the toolbox were supplied by Rumi. The production colour scheme was standardized: "Rumi" grey with a black flash on the tank and blue or green pinstriping. On the facing page, the 1951 "Turismo" offered the customers some new colours: red, black with a red tank, silver with a red tank, ivory, and ivory with a red tank. The bike had modified front forks and chrome spring boxes.

FUEL TANK CAPACITY	13 litres	LIST PRICE	198,000 lire
DRY WEIGHT	85 kg	COLOUR RANGE	all black, black partially chromed tank and white pinstriping, red with chromed tank and white pinstriping, silver with chromed tank and black pinstriping silver with chromed tank and a black upper flash, all yellow
MAXIMUM SPEED	90 km/h		
AVERAGE CONSUMPTION	3.3 litres/100 km		

"SPORT" (1950-1958)

The "Sport" model was undoubtedly the most prestigious machine in Rumi's production line-up, and it was only surpassed, after 1955, by the celebrated "Junior". After the engine had been road tested production got under way at the end of 1950, and the machine was officially presented to the public at the Milan Trade Fair in April, 1951.

The engine appeared considerably improved and was equipped with unusual Rumi-patented deflector pistons, which were later fitted to all of the models in the range. The maximum power output of the "Sport" engine was increased to 8,5 hp at 6500 rpm. The cantilever saddle and the small pillion pad were replaced by a leatherette dualseat colour-coordinated with the rest of the bike.

In 1953 a new engine was also fitted to the "Sport". The gear ratios were changed (1:17,9 for first, 1:13,00 for second, 1:9,4 for third, 1:7,46 for fourth), while the engine breathed through a Dell'Orto MB 22A carburettor. Maximum speed was increased to 105 km/h. In 1956 the cycle parts were improved as well the engine: the steel headlamp cowling was replaced by a well designed aluminium casting. The rear springing was uprated (24 mm in length) and the wheels were fitted with the indestructible "Aimon" steel rims. In that year the list price was 189.000 lire, that is to say 36.000 less than in 1950.

125 CM³ "SPORT" (1950-1958)	
ENGINE	*two-stroke, parallel flat twin*
DISPLACEMENT	*124.68 cm³*
BORE AND STROKE	*42 x 45 mm*
COMPRESSION RATIO	*7.8:1*
MAXIMUM RPM	*6,000 rpm*
MAXIMUM POWER	*7 hp (3 fiscal hp in Italy)*
CYLINDER HEADS AND BARRELS	*separate cast iron barrels; aluminium cylinder heads*
CARBURETTOR	*Dell'Orto MB 22 A with dual inlet manifold*
CARBURETTOR DATA	*choke tube 22, coupling 28.6 valve 70, jet 265, tapered needle E1, 2nd notch, max. jet 100, min. jet 45, toggle 60, float 6.5, vertical float chamber, air intake with filter*
IGNITION	*flywheel magneto with two contact breakers, two sparks per cycle, 6 V 30 W*
CLUTCH	*wet multiplate*
GEARBOX	*unit construction 4-speed constant mesh*
GEAR RATIOS	*(1950) 1st 19.4, 2nd 14.5, 3rd 10.0, 4th 7.6; (1953) 1st 26.4, 2nd 16.0, 3rd 10.8, 4th 8.57*
DRIVE	*geared primary, chain secondary*
FRAME	*open duplex cradle*
WHEELBASE	*1250 mm*
FRONT SUSPENSION	*telescopic fork with springs in the upper part*

A version of the 1954 "Sport" with an unusual faired tank that embraced the fork and the headlight; this version apparently remained at the prototype stage.

REAR SUSPENSION	*covered return springs*
WHEELS	*36 tangential wire spokes laced onto aluminium rims*
TYRES	*2.50 x 19" (optional 2.375 x 21") - front: ribbed; rear: grooved*
BRAKES	*140 mm aluminium expanding shoe brakes*
ELECTRICAL SYSTEM	*Nassetti magneto, CEV headlight, CEV rear light*
INSTRUMENTATION	*VDO speedometer reading from 0-120 km/h*

RIDING POSITION	*cantilever saddle with rear pillion pad in leather, dualseat*
FUEL TANK CAPACITY	*14 litres*
DRY WEIGHT	*90 kg*
MAXIMUM SPEED	*100 km/h*
AVERAGE CONSUMPTION	*3.4 litres/100 km*
LIST PRICE	*235,000 lire*
COLOUR RANGE	*silver with a red tank, all silver, red with a black tank flash and pinstriping, all red, Rumi grey with a black tank flash and blue and gold pinstriping*

COMPETITION SS 52 "GOBBETTO" (1951-1955)

Rumi's first year of experience with the 125 cm³ lightweight was basically positive, both in terms of commercial success and the reliability of the engine, which had been comprehensively tested in numerous trials competitions and races. These were all factors that encouraged the company to prepare a motorcycle specifically developed for racing. The objective was to provide a reliable machine blessed with a good top speed, but above all one capable of getting the best out of the sheer get-up-and-go of the two-stroke twin power unit and the lightweight frame.

The basis of the engine was unchanged, but care was taken to select the best components. As it was a two-stroke unit most attention was clearly paid to the cylinders, the transfer ports and the pistons. Cylinders in special cast iron - from 1953 the cylinders

were cast in aluminium - and aluminium pistons with special high turbulence deflectors were adopted, while the compression ratio was slightly modified. Every component of the motorcycle was carefully run-in on the Monza racing circuit for a distance of not less than 1000 kilometres.

The company supplied a special instructions with this model: the feeding mixture was to contain petrol with an octane rating of no less than 80, while the mixture was to contain al least 11% oil; specific crown wheel and pinion assemblies, supplied with the machine, were to be used for different circuits, spark plugs graded at 240 on the Bosch scale were to be used for starting and warming up the engine, whilst 300 grade plugs were specified for use during the race. It was also possible to use an alcohol-based fuel mixture but only in the works machines as the engine required particular tuning. Braking was

As well as the "Gobbetto" and "Competition", some English and French catalogues listed this bike as the "SS 52". Above, the first version of the "Gobbetto" (1951) was painted black with a red tank.

51

The "Gobbetto" seen from the left and the right. This is the specification with the Marelli ST 261 DASD external magneto, which ensured more efficient ignition.

52

The first series "Gobbetto" engine showing the chainguard (which also protected the magneto), the revcounter take-off, megaphone exhaust, and racing carbs.

The two side views of the 2nd series "Gobbetto" from 1953, with the redesigned frame; note the Standard rear shocks and the unusual tank shape. This new version of the "Gobbetto" sported ivory paintwork and a very broad yellow tank flash. The first units were fitted with the tank from the 1951 version.

was fitted with notably sturdy "Standard" dampers. As far as the engine was concerned, the cooling had been improved by the adoption of Nikasil treated aluminium barrels with a large heat dispersing area. Another stratagem designed to improve the heat dispersal capacity of the metal was to leave the crankcase surfaces unfinished. The fuel tank was replaced with a new design featuring more rounded forms, but the characteristic "Gobbetto" nickname was still used.

The colour combinations were also changed. This distinctive racing motorcycle was constructed in around 50 units before production ceased definitively in 1955. Some were exported to England, France, Sweden, Argentina and the United States of America.

taken care of by a large-diameter centrally-mounted nickel-chrome-treated aluminium front drum with twin cams and four shoes. The rear brake was of the same diameter and again had four shoes, but only a single cam.

The exhaust system was an unusual one with short, large-bore tubes that widened into authentic megaphones. On request the motorcycle could be equipped with a lighting system for use in long distance competitions. The official presentation of the model took place at the 1951 Milan Cycle and Motorcycle Show, where the specialist press dubbed it the "Gobbetto", or "Hunchback". The name derived from the unusual hump in the distinctive elongated fuel tank that extended over the steering head to incorporate the race number disc. A new version of the "Gobbetto" with various modifications appeared in 1953. The frame appeared to have been stiffened and the rear suspension

125 CM³ COMPETITION SS 52 "GOBBETTO" (1951-1955)	
ENGINE	two-stroke, horizontal twin
DISPLACEMENT	124.68 cm³
BORE AND STROKE	42 x 45 mm
COMPRESSION RATIO	10.8:1
MAXIMUM RPM	8,200 rpm
MAXIMUM POWER	9 hp
CYLINDER HEADS AND BARRELS	in special cast iron (type Z), then in aluminium; aluminium heads
CARBURETTOR	two Dell'Orto SS 23c/SS 22c units. Separate float chamber
CARBURETTOR DATA	choke tube 22, coupling 25.4, valve 70, jet 265, tapered needle R2, 3rd notch, max. jet 115, min. jet 50, float 11, float chamber type SS2, bellmouth air intake
IGNITION	flywheel magneto; some variants with external Marelli ST261-DAS-D magneto
CLUTCH	wet multiplate
GEARBOX	unit construction 4-speed constant mesh

GEAR RATIOS	*variable*
DRIVE	*geared primary, chain secondary*
FRAME	*open cradle in special lightweight tubing*
WHEELBASE	*1265 mm*
FRONT SUSPENSION	*leading link forks*
REAR SUSPENSION	*plunger box type - 2nd series: s/arm*
WHEELS	*36 spokes laced onto aluminium rims, front 18", rear 17"*
TYRES	*front: ribbed 2.00 x 18"; rear: grooved 2.50 x 17" (racing type)*
BRAKES	*front: central expanding brake with four shoes, twin operating cams ø; rear: central expanding brake*
ELECTRICAL SYSTEM	*Nassetti flywheel magneto 6V-30W*
INSTRUMENTATION	*rev counter calibrated 1:10,000 incorporated in the fuel tank*
RIDING POSITION	*racing saddle in suede leather*
FUEL TANK CAPACITY	*22 litres (aluminium tank)*
DRY WEIGHT	*1st series with cast iron cylinders without external magneto - 83 kg*
MAXIMUM SPEED	*from 128 to 136 km/h depending on the version and the fuel used*
AVERAGE CONSUMPTION	*depended on the specification*
LIST PRICE	*470,000 lire ex-works including equipment*
COLOUR RANGE	*1951, black with a red tank; 1953, Rumi grey with yellow design on the tank*

A nice overhead view that highlights the sleek styling of the "Gobbetto".

Some details of the 2nd series "Gobbetto". Right, a close up of the tank, with the built-in revcounter, and the handlebars; note the brake lever with the dual control for the front brake. Below, left, the engine with its stubby megaphones and external magneto; right, the rear fork.

56

The first version of the "Scoiattolo" was introduced at the 1951 Milan Show. The "Scoiattolo", conceived by Rumi as a motorcycle-cum-scooter, offered both comfort and protection to rider and passenger alike.

"SCOIATTOLO" ("SQUIRREL") (1951-1957)

The Milan Trade Fair, this time the 1951 edition, was again the setting for the presentation of a Rumi product, the "Scoiattolo". Rumi's objective was to launch a utilitarian vehicle that represented an ideal compromise between motorcycle and scooter design, capable of offering the rider a high degree of protection and notably high level of general comfort. The "Scoiattolo" met this specification in full. The machine's enclosed chassis, apart from covering all the mechanical components, provided full weather protection for the rider, whilst the 14-inch wheels and the particular conformation of the chassis ensured that it was an extremely user-friendly bike to ride.

On the mechanical side, the crankcase was basically the same as that used in the "Turismo" and "Sport" models. The only difference concerned the design of the halfcasings, which had been modified to provide mounting points for the pressed steel bodyshell. The heel and toe rocking foot change featured an unusual intermediate control that allowed the rocker pedal to be transferred below the generously proportioned running board. In 1953 the machine was improved with the adoption of a new engine and four-speed gearbox that provided a higher maximum power output. A V.D.O. speedometer-odometer scaled from 0-100 km/h was incorporated into the headlamp cowling, and the scooter was fitted with a teledraulic front fork. In the same year a version with electric starting was also presented. In spite of the fact that the bike did not achieve the degree of commercial success that it merited, the electric starting system should nevertheless be considered a minor masterpiece of electrical engineering in the best Rumi tradition.

In the "Scoiattolo" the dynamotor not only functioned as the starter motor, but also as a generator, and was run directly off the left-hand extremity of the crankshaft, where it also doubled as a flywheel. As this design did not make it possible to fit reduction gearing its use had to be restricted to small two-stroke engines; it was, however an economical and reliable device. Electrical power was guaranteed by two 6V batteries connected in parallel, and starting was a matter of pressing a button placed on the handlebar.

In 1953 the electric start "Scoiattolo" cost 218,000 lire ex-works, whilst the kick-start version cost 20,000 lire less in the same year. The ex-works price actually dropped to 168,000 lire in 1957, the last year of production for this motorcycle-scooter.

125 CM³ "SCOIATTOLO" (1951-1957)	
ENGINE	*two-stroke, horizontal twin*
DISPLACEMENT	*124.68 cm³*
BORE AND STROKE	*42 x 45 mm*
COMPRESSION RATIO	*6.5:1*
MAXIMUM RPM	*4,800 rpm*
MAXIMUM POWER	*6 hp (3 fiscal hp in Italy)*
CYLINDER HEADS AND BARRELS	*two separate cast iron barrels; aluminium cylinder heads*
CARBURETTOR	*Dell'Orto UA 15 S*
CARBURETTOR DATA	*choke tube 15, coupling M23, valve 55, jet 262, tapered needle C7, 2nd notch, max. jet 60, min. jet 45, toggle 58, float 7.5, vertical float chamber, air intake with filter*
IGNITION	*Nassetti 6V 30 W flywheel magneto with twin spark*
CLUTCH	*wet multiplate*
GEARBOX	*unit construction 3-speed constant mesh, later a 4-speed unit*
GEAR RATIOS	*1st 26.4, 2nd 16.0, 3rd 10.8, 4th 8.57*
DRIVE	*geared primary, chain secondary*
FRAME	*pressed-steel monocoque*
WHEELBASE	*1200 mm*
FRONT SUSPENSION	*telescopic fork with guides and springs in the upper part*
REAR SUSPENSION	*swinging arm with hydraulic damper*

WHEELS	28 tangential spokes laced onto iron rims, removable spindles
TYRES	grooved 3.25 x 14" at front and rear
BRAKES	130 mm ø central expanding shoe brakes
ELECTRICAL SYSTEM	CEV 105 headlight, CEV rear light and horn
INSTRUMENTATION	originally not provided, later fitted with a VDO speedometer calibrated from 1-100 km/h

RIDING POSITION	leatherette dualseat
FUEL TANK CAPACITY	6 litres, giving a range of 180 km
DRY WEIGHT	105 kg
MAXIMUM SPEED	80 km/h
AVERAGE CONSUMPTION	35 km/litre
LIST PRICE	217,000 lire ex-works
COLOUR RANGE	Light grey 8126L, blue

On the facing page, top, the 1951 version of the "Scoiattolo"; note the bodywork which, as well as enclosing the mechanical units, protected the rider from the elements; below, a close up of the tank and handlebars of the 1953 "Scoiattolo": the speedometer-odometer recessed into the headlamp cowling was missing from the previous version. This page, left, a partial view of the new 4-speed power unit and the single HT coil ignition fitted to the 1953 "Scoiattolo".

Right, the "Scoiattolo" was also available with an aluminium Durapid sidecar with a 3.25 wheel. Below, a side view of the 1953 "Scoiattolo".

A three-quarters view of the "Scoiattolo". In 1953 the price of the bike with the electric starter was 218,000 lire ex-works; in that same year the price of the kickstart version was 198,000 lire.

"REGOLARITÀ" (1952-1954 1ST AND 2ND SERIES)

On the basis of the promising results obtained in trials events during the previous season using the standard "Sport" model, in 1952 Rumi decided to prepare a purpose-built motorcycle for the extremely demanding off-road races. It was decided to start off with the "Gobbetto" frame, which was considered to be notably more robust than the standard chassis. The first machines specifically designed for trials competition where therefore assembled around this base with all the special features required by this particular sport: QD wheel spindles to facilitate tyre changes; reinforced telescopic front forks; tubular shielding for the pedal cranks; and lowered gear ratios to favour low speed engine performance.
The machines prepared to this specification were reserved for the works riders and were not produced commercially. They obtained gratifying results in both national and international competition.
In the spring of 1953, as production of a new engine got underway, an up-dated model, derived from the standard "Sport "version, was introduced and remained in the Rumi catalogue until 1955, the year in which the "Six Day" version appeared. This was a machine that had received more through preparation with trials competition in mind. Rumi was among the first motorcycle manufacturers to see the advantage of designing and constructing machines specifically for trials competition. The "Six Day" model was to remain in the Rumi catalogue for five consecutive years, but relatively few examples were produced and almost all of them were destined for the works team. This model's lack of success can be attributed to the fact that, even in those years, dedicated trials specialists were already turning towards four-stroke engines constructed by the more famous motorcycle manufacturers. Rumi was left with the honour of having launched the idea of the specialist trial bike.

125 CM³ "REGOLARITÀ" (1952-1954) 1st and 2nd series	
ENGINE	*two-stroke, horizontal twin*
DISPLACEMENT	*124.68 cm³*
BORE AND STROKE	*42 x 45 mm*
COMPRESSION RATIO	*7.8:1*
MAXIMUM RPM	*6,000 rpm*

The first bike specially designed by Rumi for trials competition (1952). Based on the "Gobbetto" frame this machine was fitted with a larger 130 mm headlamp, QD wheels, raised mudguards, legshields, etc. In this photo, taken on the 6th June 1952 during the fourth Scudo del Sud event, the 1st series "Regolarità" is surrounded by members of the Rumi team who, with the exception of Guglielmo Strada, all came in first equal.

In spring 1953 the arrival of new forks and a new engine signalled the birth of an updated 2nd series "Regolarità" (derived directly from the "Sport"), which remained in production until 1955.

Another shot of the 2nd series "Regolarità". Apart from a specially prepared engine, the particular specification reserved for the works team bikes included different cycle parts, QD wheels, raised handlebars and reinforced suspension.

Details of the 1st series "Regolarità". Top left, the air bottle was fitted at the rear on the right hand side. Right, part of the engine and the carburettor.

MAXIMUM POWER	*7 hp (3 fiscal hp in Italy)*
CYLINDER HEADS AND BARRELS	*two separate barrels, in special Z cast iron; aluminium cylinder heads*
CARBURETTOR	*Dell'Orto MB 22A with dual inlet manifold*
CARBURETTOR DATA	*choke tube 22, coupling 28.6, valve 70, jet 265, tapered needle E1, 2nd notch, max. jet 100, min. jet 45, toggle 60, float 7.5, vertical float chamber, air intake with filter*
IGNITION	*flywheel magneto with two contact breakers, two sparks per cycle, 6 V 30 W*
CLUTCH	*wet multiplate*
GEARBOX	*unit construction 4-speed constant mesh*
GEAR RATIOS	*1952 model ratios unknown; 1953 model ratios as per the "Sport"*
DRIVE	*geared primary, chain secondary*
FRAME	*reinforced racing type tubular open duplex cradle*
WHEELBASE	*1230 mm*
FRONT SUSPENSION	*reinforced teledraulic fork*
REAR SUSPENSION	*covered return springs with extensive travel*
WHEELS	*36 spokes laced onto iron rims*
TYRES	*2.50 x 19" grooved with special block tread*
BRAKES	*140 mm ø aluminium expanding shoe brakes front and rear*
ELECTRICAL SYSTEM	*Nassetti magneto; 130 ø CEV headlight; rear light; horn*
INSTRUMENTATION	*not fitted*
RIDING POSITION	*leatherette single-seater saddle; tool bag, parcel rack*
FUEL TANK CAPACITY	*14 litres*
DRY WEIGHT	*98 kg*
MAXIMUM SPEED	*90 km/h*
AVERAGE CONSUMPTION	*depended on the specification*
LIST PRICE	*not declared*
COLOUR RANGE	*1952, silver with a red tank; 1953, Rumi grey with black tank flash and blue pinstriping*

"BICARBURATORE" (1953-1956)

The manufacturer considered the "Bicarburatore" ("twin carburettor") to be the hot version of the "Sport", and on Rumi's request the National Sporting Commission of the Italian Motorcycling Federation homologated it for use in Division 3 racing. At the time of its launch it was known, for a mixture of commercial motives and local habit, under a number of different names: "Gran Sport", "2 Carburettor", "Super Sport T.T.", and "Amatore", or "Amateur".

Production got underway in the July of 1953 with two versions on offer: the "Velocità" had two Dell'Orto carburettors with 18 mm choke tubes, single float chamber and twin air filters, and optional 19 or 21 inch diameter wheels, while the "Amatore" had two Dell'Orto carburettors with 22 mm choke tubes, bellmouth air intakes and separate float chambers. The wheels

were again either 19 or 21 inches with either "Aimon" steel or aluminium rims. These versions were fitted with a suede leather or leatherette dualseat, colour matched to blend with the overall colour scheme. Like all the saddles fitted to Rumi motorcycles, it was produced by the M.G. firm of Bergamo.

A version with an 18 litre fuel tank for use in long-distance endurance events was introduced in 1955, whilst some of the machines raced by the works team were fitted with external magnetos and up-rated electrical systems. Again in 1955, an engine with aluminium K.S. cylinder barrel replaced by the old cast iron barrels.

Numerous successes were obtained with this extremely versatile model, both by the Rumi works team and by privateers. The most demanding races in which the machines were used were undoubtedly the Milano-Taranto and the Motorcycling Giro d'Italia.

In 1953 Rumi began building the "Bicarburatore" model. Considered a tweaked version of the "Sport", this bike was available in two versions: the "Velocità" and the "Amatore", shown in the photo. Some catalogues also listed it as the SS (Super Sport).

A detail of the engine fitted to the "Amatore"; note the two 22 mm Dell'Orto with the stubby vertical bellmouths and the separate "Competizione"-type float chamber.

125 CM³ "BICARBURATORE" (1953-1956)	
ENGINE	*two-stroke twin*
DISPLACEMENT	*124.68 cm³*
BORE AND STROKE	*42 x 45 mm*
COMPRESSION RATIO	*10.5:1*
MAXIMUM RPM	*7,300 rpm*
MAXIMUM POWER	*9 hp (3 fiscal hp in Italy)*
CYLINDER HEADS AND BARRELS	*in special Z-type cast iron, aluminium heads; later fitted with aluminium cylinders*
CARBURETTOR	*two Dell'Orto UB 18s, UB 22s on request*
CARBURETTOR DATA	*UB 22: choke tube 22, coupling M 28.6, valve 70, jet 265, tapered needle E1, 2nd notch, max. jet 90, min. jet 45, toggle 58, float 7.5, separate float chamber, racing type air intake*
IGNITION	*flywheel magneto with two contact breakers, two sparks per cycle, 6 V 30 W*
CLUTCH	*wet multiplate*
GEARBOX	*unit construction 4-speed constant mesh*
GEAR RATIOS	*1st 24.0, 2nd 17.3, 3rd 12.6, 4th 10.0*

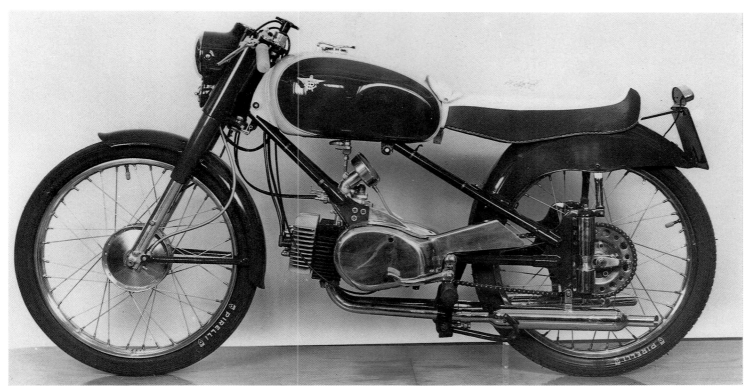

Left, the classic "Velocità" version of the "Bicarburatore" was fitted with two 18 mm Dell'Orto carbs sharing a single central float chamber. Note the typical oval filter connecting the two air intakes. Below, the 1953 version of the "Bicarburatore" with iron rims; the silver livery with the red tank was first seen on the "Sport".

Top right and centre, the long distance competition version of the "Bicarburatore" from 1955. This bike had aluminium cylinders, a front fork with an integral cast aluminium headlight cowling, larger rear shock absorbers, an 18-litre tank and iron Aimon rims. Bottom, the "Bicarburatore" imported by Svecia of Stockholm for the Swedish market: between 1953 and 1956 about 300 units were exported to Sweden.

DRIVE	geared primary, chain secondary
FRAME	open duplex cradle
WHEELBASE	1240 mm
FRONT SUSPENSION	teledraulic fork with covered upper guides and springs
REAR SUSPENSION	covered return springs
WHEELS	36 spokes laced onto aluminium rims, second series used Aimon steel rims
TYRES	2.75 x 21" (optional 2.50 x 19") - front: ribbed; rear: groo ed
BRAKES	140 mm ø aluminium expanding shoe brakes
ELECTRICAL SYSTEM	Nassetti magneto, CEV 105 headlight, CEV rear light
INSTRUMENTATION	VDO speedometer calibrated from 1-140 km/h
RIDING POSITION	1st series with cantilever saddle, second series with leather dualseat
FUEL TANK CAPACITY	13 litres; 18 litres on request
DRY WEIGHT	84 kg
MAXIMUM SPEED	115 km/h; max. incline 25%
AVERAGE CONSUMPTION	depending on the specification
LIST PRICE	250,000 lire ex-works
COLOUR RANGE	silver with a red tank, red, red with a white tank flash and black pinstriping, red with a black tank flash and white pinstriping, red with a black design on the sides of the tank and gold pinstriping, Rumi grey with a black tank flash and blue pinstriping

"G.T. - GRANTURISMO" (1953-1956)

As far as motorcycle production went, 1953 was definitely Rumi's best year, and in the circumstances the company wanted to add a larger capacity motorcycle to its catalogue in order to capture a slice of the medium-capacity bike market. The classic flat twin was suitably redesigned by Ing. Salmaggi, and mounted in a robust frame equipped with leading link forks and rear swinging arm. The capacious fuel tank was extended to enclose the steering head as well as the headlight.

An instrument panel was set into the tank itself and contained an ammeter, a clock and speedometer-odometer, following the example set by the large capacity British and American touring machines. The speedo drive was taken directly from the gearbox.

As usual the machine was presented in the spring, at the Milan Trade Fair, although a prototype version had already taken part in a number of long distance races. The G.T.'s career in trial event, on the other hand, was insignificant as it was found to be too heavy and insufficiently agile.

Rumi did not use its anvil anchor trade mark for the 200 GT, preferring to decorate the fuel tank with a facsimile of Donnino Rumi's signature in either white or grey according to the colour of the bike. The cylinder capacity was indicated on the front mudguard fin.

Later versions had the Rumi name painted on the tank in white on a circular black background. Probably for tax reasons, a 175 cm³ version of the G.T. was also offered.

With all character and good breeding of the 200, this was a motorcycle with a certain touch of class that offered good performance as well as excellent styling. But the 200 GT never obtained the degree of success that it deserved, perhaps because it was competing in a market that was already well served by the more famous motorcycle manufacturers. Penalized on the one hand by the high costs imposed by its quality engineering, and on the other by the popularity enjoyed by certain well known contemporary 250 singles, the 200 G.T. went out of production in 1956.

The 200 cm³ "Gran Turismo" was presented in 1953 and targeted at fans of larger capacity bikes. Note the tank badge (inspired by Donnino Rumi's signature) and the indication of the engine capacity on the front mudguard.

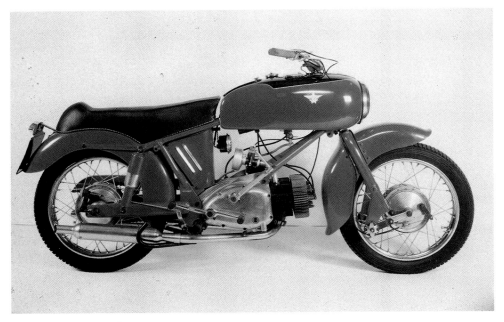

The "Gran Turismo" from the right hand side. On the facing page, the prototype of the "Formichino" was introduced at the 1954 Milan Trade Fair. The most obvious difference between this and the series produced machine was the monoarm front suspension. Despite the initial publicity dedicated to it, only a very few units of this version were produced.

200 CM³ G.T. "GRANTURISMO" (1953-1956)

ENGINE	two-stroke, flat twin
DISPLACEMENT	196.12 cm³
BORE AND STROKE	49 x 52 mm
COMPRESSION RATIO	not declared
MAXIMUM RPM	6,000 rpm
MAXIMUM POWER	10,6 hp (4 fiscal hp in Italy)
CYLINDER HEADS AND BARRELS	separate cast iron barrels; aluminium cylinder heads
CARBURETTOR	Dell'Orto UB 24S with filter
CARBURETTOR DATA	choke tube 24, coupling M 28.6, valve 70, jet 265, tapered needle E1, 2nd notch, max. jet 105, min. jet 45, toggle 58, float 6.5, vertical float chamber, air intake with filter
IGNITION	distributor, 100 W flywheel - alternator 6 V - 14 ah battery
CLUTCH	wet multiplate
GEARBOX	unit construction 4-speed constant mesh
GEAR RATIOS	1st 24.6, 2nd 16.0, 3rd 10.8, 4th 8.57
DRIVE	geared primary, chain secondary with anti-snatch device
FRAME	tubular steel triangulated on both sides
WHEELBASE	1320 mm
FRONT SUSPENSION	leading link forks and return springs
REAR SUSPENSION	swinging arm with Standard oil-filled dampers
WHEELS	36 spokes laced onto steel rims, removable rear spindle; QD type at front
TYRES	3.00 x 17" block tread
BRAKES	170 mm ø expanding shoe brakes at front and rear
ELECTRICAL SYSTEM	distributor, 130 ø CEV headlight, CEV rear light 100W
INSTRUMENTATION	panel on the tank containing ammeter, clock and VDO speedometer calibrated from 1-140 km/h
RIDING POSITION	two-tone dualseat
FUEL TANK CAPACITY	20 litres
DRY WEIGHT	110 kg
MAXIMUM SPEED	110 km/h
AVERAGE CONSUMPTION	30 km/litre
LIST PRICE	280,000 lire ex-works
COLOUR RANGE	Rumi grey with a black tank flash, blue and amaranth red pinstriping with a grey design on the tank and green pinstriping; red with a black tank flash and white pinstriping, amaranth red with ivory tank flash and blue pinstriping, ivory with an amaranth tank flash and green pinstriping

"FORMICHINO" (1954-1960)

The launch of the "Formichino" took place in 1954 and, according to Rumi's plans, the machine was to take the company into the newly formed scooter sector, dominated at that time by Piaggio with the "Vespa" and Innocenti with the "Lambretta". The styling of this splendid scooter was undoubtedly the work of Donnino Rumi, and demonstrated all his artistic talent. They say that he built a life-size clay model around an engine mounted on trestles. The stressed aluminium alloy bodywork was essentially divided into two parts: the front, divided in turn into two shells, which incorporated the front forks, the headlight, and the fuel tank; and the rear section, which constituted the seat base and the mudguard over the driven wheel. The production of the aluminium castings was handled by the Metalpress company of Bergamo. The firm was part of the Rumi industrial group and specialized in diecasting techniques.

The engine was intelligently located at the centre of the machine and acted as a stress member connecting the two chassis elements. It was equipped right from the start with a four-speed gearbox and the same engine that was used to power the contemporary "Sport" and "Turismo" models, a fact that did a lot to simplify production processes. Deliveries began in July 1954 and the first examples put into circulation were fitted with a single leading link front suspension system. This was a very well made but expensive feature and subsequent standard production models adopted a fork with two lower leading links.

In 1956 modifications were made to the rear section of the bodywork, which was split into two parts instead of being formed from a single casting. A Veglia speedometer-odometer was mounted on the handlebar. A year later the Milan Trade Fair was again the setting for the presentation of the "Sport" model, distinguished by new aluminium cylinder barrels and a carburettor with a 22 mm choke tube; in this form the engine's power output rose to 8 hp and the top speed to 105 km/h.

The "Formichino" range was further extended in 1958 when new versions were introduced alongside the "Normale" (Standard) and "Sport". The "ST-EC" model featured pressed steel bodywork, a tubular frame and a tubular steel front fork. The EC part of the name stood for "Economical", and in fact the scooter was sold for just 125,000 lire. Only a few hundred examples were produced, mostly destined for export markets. This version was painted British Racing Green with white stripes on the tank.

Three views of the 1954 "Formichino": the aluminium alloy stressed body was basically divided into a front and a rear section; note the front seat support, which was an integral part of the bodywork casting. A steel version of this component was later bolted onto the body. On the facing page, a detail of a disassembled Dell'Orto UA 15S carb: note the particular form of the filter with the downwards facing air intake.

74

The "Formichino Lusso" was practically the same as the standard model but was equipped with a number of accessories such a dualseat, cast aluminium footrests for the passenger, chromed hubcaps and a chrome strip on the rear mudguard. On request it could be equipped with 3.50 x 10" tyres, and the colour range was considerably widened.

Following the successes obtained at Monthléry, in the 1957 and 1958 Bol d'Or events, the scooter was also offered in a special "Bol d'Or" edition. This version was specifically prepared for endurance races and, not surprisingly, it was painted gold. The engine developed 8.5 hp at 7200 rpm, a degree of performance that was achieved by fitting special chrome-barrelled aluminium cylinders, as well as two Dell'Orto 18 mm carburettors. On request the machine could also be supplied with 22 mm carburettors. Improved suspension was also fitted to this model, as were 3.50 x 10" tyres and a supplementary fuel tank.

Tank decals on the "Sport" and "Bol d'Or" versions included the usual Rumi trademark plus the Italian flag, as on the competition models. Again in 1958, a version fitted with a 149.9 cm³ engine was introduced throughout the model range. This unit had a bore of 46 mm and a stroke of 45 mm and developed 9 hp at 6500 rpm. In 1959 the "Normale" model remained in production unchanged, whilst the "Sport" was fitted with the chrome-barrelled aluminium cylinders and shod with 3.50 x 10" tyres as standard equipment. production of the "Formichino" only ceased when the motorcycle division of the Fonderie Officine Rumi finally closed down.

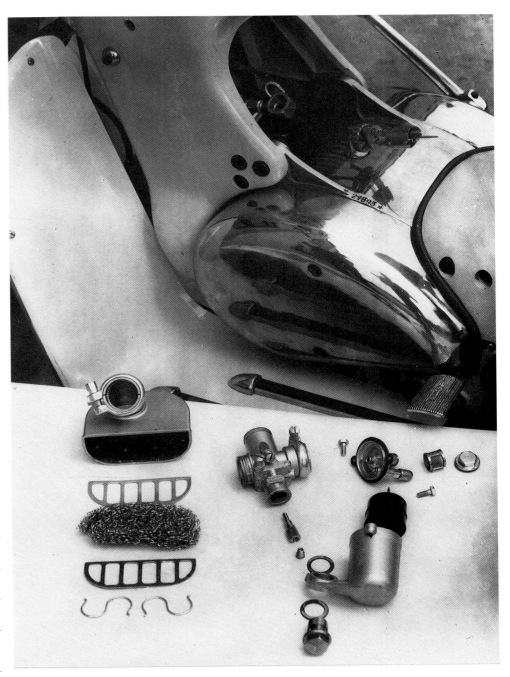

125 CM³ "FORMICHINO" (1954-1960)	
ENGINE	two-stroke, flat twin
DISPLACEMENT	124.68 cm³
BORE AND STROKE	42 x 45 mm
COMPRESSION RATIO	6.5:1
MAXIMUM RPM	6,000 rpm
MAXIMUM POWER	6.5 hp (3 fiscal hp in Italy)
CYLINDER HEADS AND BARRELS	cast iron

CARBURETTOR	*Dell'Orto UA 15S, with special hemispherical filter; carburettor for Sport model MB 22A*
CARBURETTOR DATA	*choke tube 15, coupling M23, valve 55, jet 262, tapered needle C7, 2nd notch, max. jet 60, min. jet 45, toggle 58, float 7.5, vertical float chamber, air intake with filter*
IGNITION	*flywheel magneto with two contact breakers, two sparks per cycle*
CLUTCH	*wet multiplate*
GEARBOX	*unit construction 4-speed constant mesh*
GEAR RATIOS	*1st 26.4, 2nd 16.0, 3rd 10.8, 4th 8.57*
DRIVE	*geared primary, chain secondary running under a fully enclosed chainguard*
FRAME	*stressed bodywork cast in special A.R. aluminium alloy*
WHEELBASE	*1200 mm*
FRONT SUSPENSION	*leading links and damper springs*
REAR SUSPENSION	*s/arm and built-in chaincase with rubber dampers*
WHEELS	*two-piece steel pressings; interchangeable; spare wheel*
TYRES	*4.00 x 8" beaded, Sport 3.50 x 10"*
BRAKES	*ø 125 front and rear*
ELECTRICAL SYSTEM	*Nassetti magneto, CEV swivelling headlight, CEV rear light*
INSTRUMENTATION	*not fitted at first, then Veglia VDO speedometer calibrated from 1-100 km/h*
RIDING POSITION	*cantilever saddle in black leatherette, dualseat for the Sport*

Above, below and on the facing page, three views of the 1955 "Formichino", produced until 1956. After that year the rear fairing was divided into two parts: a central casting, fixed to the engine, and the "tail", which doubled as a mudguard.

Above and right, two shots of the "Formichino ST-EC" which, introduced in 1958, was built in 125 and 175 cm³ versions with metal bodywork over a stressed tubular steel frame.

FUEL TANK CAPACITY	*7 litres*
DRY WEIGHT	*100 kg*
MAXIMUM SPEED	*75 km/h; max. gradient 20%*
AVERAGE CONSUMPTION	*2.5 litres petrol/100 km*
LIST PRICE	*138,000 lire ex-works*
COLOUR RANGE	*ivory, yellow ivory, Rumi grey, silver, white-gold, sky blue, rosso corsa, blue corsa, British racing green for the ST-EC model*

"REGOLARITÀ SEI GIORNI" (1955-1960)

In the spring of 1954, in view of the works entry for the murderously tough international Six Day Trial event (held in Britain in that year), Ing. Guidorossi prepared a motorcycle that can be considered as the prototype of the "Regolarità Sei Giorni" ("Six Days Trial") model that entered the Rumi catalogue the following year. Its unexpected success in its debut event - four entries, four gold medals - encouraged the Rumi engineering staff to follow up the project they had started.

It was probably the first time in motorcycling history that a machine had been designed and produced expressly for off-road competition. the frame, made of light, variable diameter tubing, was a triangulated structure that gradually widened on its way from the steering head to the rear swinging arm; the engine was mounted cantilever style from the centre. The motorcycle was equipped with knobbly tyres on both wheels, which in turn were provided with QD spindles to facilitate changing and repairing the tyres. The Earles-type front fork with long leading links, clearly inspired by British machines, was very rigid and provided notable wheel travel. It was later replaced by traditional teledraulic forks, which undoubtedly responded better to the stresses imposed by off-road riding. Rear suspension was taken care by a swinging arm and efficient, cylindrically sleeved Sturcher hydraulic struts.

The "Sei Giorni" version of the "Regolarità": note the upswept engine, set high to improve ground clearance, and high handlebars for the ideal riding position during competition.

79

The exhaust fitted to the "Sei Giorni" were decidedly upswept; the quickly detachable made for rapid tyre changes.

125 CM³ "REGOLARITÀ SEI GIORNI" (1955-1960)	
ENGINE	two-stroke, horizontal twin
DISPLACEMENT	124.68 cm³
BORE AND STROKE	42 x 45 mm
COMPRESSION RATIO	10.5:1
MAXIMUM RPM	7,300 rpm
MAXIMUM POWER	9 hp (3 fiscal hp in Italy)

CYLINDER HEADS AND BARRELS	in special aluminium, aluminium cylinder heads
CARBURETTOR	Dell'Orto MB 22 A with dual inlet manifold
CARBURETTOR DATA	choke tube 22, coupling M 28.6, valve 70, jet 265, tapered needle E1, 2nd notch, max. jet 100, min. jet 45, toggle 60, float 6.5, float chamber, air intake with filter
IGNITION	flywheel magneto with two contact breakers, two sparks per cycle, 6 V 30 W

Left, a bike with its race number and tool kit. Below, a detail of the robust hydraulically damped telescopic fork fitted in place of the Earles type; note the rubber gaiters over the external springs.

81

CLUTCH	*wet multiplate*
GEARBOX	*unit construction 4-speed*
GEAR RATIOS	*1st 26.4, 2nd 16.0, 3rd 10.8, 4th 8.5*
DRIVE	*geared primary, chain secondary*
FRAME	*reinforced lightweight tubular triangulated in both sides*
WHEELBASE	*not declared*
FRONT SUSPENSION	*Earles fork with Sturcher dampers (telescopic on request)*
REAR SUSPENSION	*swinging arm with sleeved Sturcher dampers*
WHEELS	*36 spokes laced onto reinforced steel rims, extractable spindles*
TYRES	*2.50 x 18" beaded*
BRAKES	*175 mm ø expanding shoe brakes front and rear*
ELECTRICAL SYSTEM	*Nassetti magneto, ø 130 CEV headlight with three lamps, horn, rear light*
INSTRUMENTATION	*not fitted*
RIDING POSITION	*special saddle in black leatherette, leather tool bag*
FUEL TANK CAPACITY	*18 litres*
DRY WEIGHT	*92 kg*
MAXIMUM SPEED	*100 km/h; max gradient 30%*
AVERAGE CONSUMPTION	*depending on the specification*
LIST PRICE	*not declared*
COLOUR RANGE	*Rumi grey with a black tank flash and blue pinstriping.*

One of the four Rumi "Regolaritàs" built in the Spring of 1954 with a view to the marque's taking part in the International Six Days Trial event in England: these four bikes amount to pre-series versions of the 1955 "Sei Giorni" model. As can be seen, the frame design is practically identical to the definitive version; the fork was still the classic component mounted on the 2nd series "Regolarità" from 1953.

The definitive version of the prototype of the "Junior" with the Earles forks. The photo shows the experimental lug (with a good five drillings) at the end of the thrust arm, which was used in a bid to find the best configuration.

"JUNIOR" (1955-1959)

Plans to build a sporting motorcycle with sparkling performance, which could be homologated for use in Div.3 racing, took concrete form in 1955. The "Twin Carburettor" model, powered by the new engine, had proved more than satisfactory from the points of view of power and reliability, and it seemed that only slight modifications would be necessary in order to boost performance even more. On the other hand the frame soon showed that it had its limitations, as the rear suspension system was clearly inadequate.

Ing. Guidorossi therefore took a selection of tubular elements of varying diameters and designed a new open cradle frame triangulated on both sides. The frame was completed with a rear swinging arm and well-designed Earles-type front fork, and four-shoe brakes. As some riders considered this Earles fork to be too flexible laterally, the bike was also offered with the teledraulic fork

from the "Sport", but with the sleeves slightly shortened. The aluminium fuel tank was notably capacious at 18 litres, and was based on a clay model made by Donnino Rumi himself. The result was an aesthetically attractive and functionally efficient component.

The "Junior" benefited from two virtually contemporaneous official presentations, at the XXVIth Turin Cycle and Motorcycle Exhibition, and at the Milan Trade Fair. In both cases it met with considerable critical approval. From the start of production the engine was equipped with the new chrome-barrelled aluminium cylinders and German-built K.S. deflector pistons. The engine could be fitted on request with 18, 20, or 22 mm carburettors, the last of these having a notably large separate float chamber.

In 1956 an unusual version of the "Junior" was introduced for export to Sweden. According to the road traffic legislation of that country the weight of the machine was not to exceed 70 kg, including the fuel. Therefore lightweight, lateral expansion-type drum

84

The 1955 version of the "Junior" had "Sport"-type teledraulic forks with slightly shorter forks covers; some riders preferred this design to the Earles forks, considered too elastic laterally. The tank was decorated with the characteristic black motif, both on models painted in "Rumi" grey and red.

brakes, a magnesium crankcase, "Standard" dampers in place of the classic Sturcher items, and 2.00 x 19" wheels were fitted. Weight-saving aluminium chambers were welded into the fuel tank, which restricted its capacity to 5 litres. In the same year the Rumi "Junior" obtained FMI-OTS homologation as a "Sport class" machine with the following equipment: two 18 mm carburettors with 16.5 mm inlet manifolds, teledraulic front forks, and 2.50 x 19" tyres. The UA 18 mm carburettors were specified with a minimum jet of 45 and maximum jet of 78/80 and 80/85. Slight improvements made to the cylinders in 1958 boosted power output to 10 hp at 8500 rpm, but the rest of the engine remained unchanged until 1959, the year in which the "Junior" was replaced by the "Gentleman". As it was a motorcycle with decidedly sporting features and a relatively high purchase price, it was clearly not produced in great numbers.

125 CM³ "JUNIOR" (1955-1959)

ENGINE	two-stroke, horizontal twin
DISPLACEMENT	124.68 cm³
BORE AND STROKE	42 x 45 mm
COMPRESSION RATIO	10.5:1
MAXIMUM RPM	7,300-8,000 rpm
MAXIMUM POWER	9 hp (3 fiscal hp in Italy)
CYLINDER HEADS AND BARRELS	in special aluminium with aluminium cylinder heads
CARBURETTOR	Dell'Orto UA 18 Dx-Sx
CARBURETTOR DATA	choke tube 18, coupling M23, valve 60, jet 262, tapered needle C1, 2nd notch, max. jet 78, min. jet 45, toggle 58, float 7.5, separate float chamber, racing-type air intake
IGNITION	flywheel magneto with two contact breakers, two sparks per cycle, 6 V 30 W
CLUTCH	wet multiplate
GEARBOX	unit construction 4-speed constant mesh
GEAR RATIOS	1st 24.0, 2nd 17.3, 3rd 12.6, 4th 10.0
DRIVE	geared primary, chain secondary

FRAME	*in lightweight special steel tubing*
WHEELBASE	*1250 mm with a telescopic fork, 1220 mm with an Earles fork*
FRONT SUSPENSION	*teledraulic fork, Earles fork with Sturcher dampers*
REAR SUSPENSION	*swinging arm with Sturcher dampers*
WHEELS	*36 spokes laced onto reinforced aluminium rims*
TYRES	*Pirelli 2.50 x 19" - front: ribbed; rear: grooved*
BRAKES	*140 mm ø aluminium expanding shoe front brake (170 ø expanding type with four shoes with the Earles fork); 160 mm ø expanding rear brake*
ELECTRICAL SYSTEM	*6 V 30 W Nassetti magneto, CEV 130 headlight, rear light, horn*
INSTRUMENTATION	*not fitted*
RIDING POSITION	*black leather saddle and pad on fuel tank*
FUEL TANK CAPACITY	*18 litres*
DRY WEIGHT	*82 kg, 72 kg for the export model including lubricants*
MAXIMUM SPEED	*115 km/h when fitted with a silencer, 130 with a megaphone exhaust, max. gradient 25%*
AVERAGE CONSUMPTION	*depending on the specification*
LIST PRICE	*275,000 lire ex-works*
COLOUR RANGE	*red with a black design on the tank and silver pinstriping, Rumi grey with a black design on the tank and silver pinstriping, red with black tank side panels. Export models were red with a white design on the tank and black pinstriping.*

Testing a "Junior" Earles inside the Rumi works in Bergamo. The racing "Junior", like the "Gobbetto", was delivered after a 100 km running period, carried out by Rumi testers so that the bike could be used in competition immediately.

"DIANA" (1955-1958)

In 1955 the "Turismo" model was dropped from the Rumi catalogue and replaced by the "Diana" as it was hoped to revitalize sales with a moderately priced new motorcycle that was quite unlike the previous model.

The frame was redesigned from scratch and featured a traditional layout with telescopic front forks, and a rear swinging arm with hydraulic dampers. The engine was, of course, the classic flat twin that had powered the previous models, and was fitted to both the "Turismo" and the "Sport" version introduced in 1957. As fitted to the latter bike it developed 8 hp running on a compression ratio of 10.5:1, good enough for a maximum speed at 105 km/h. The "Diana" was presented on two separate occasions in 1956: the Milan Spring Trade Fair,

and the Cycle and Motorcycle Show, also held in Milan that December. The quality of the finish and fittings appeared inferior to Rumi's customary standards. Bolts and various accessories, for example, were in galvanized steel rather than chromed; "Standard" dampers and steel wheel rims were fitted, and so on. This policy allowed the list price to be kept down to 180,000 lire, whilst the original 1950 "Turismo" model had cost 198,000.

In 1958 the "Puma" appeared in Rumi's catalogue for the first time. This model was available in "Turismo" and "Sport" versions whose frames and general architecture were identical to those of the "Diana". The "Puma" was offered with a choice of two engine capacities, 125 or 175 cm^3, but it seems that it was never mass produced and probably never got beyond the prototype stage.

125 CM³ "DIANA" (1955-1958)

ENGINE	*two-stroke, horizontal twin*
DISPLACEMENT	*124.68 cm³*
BORE AND STROKE	*42 x 45 mm*
COMPRESSION RATIO	*6:1*
MAXIMUM RPM	*5,800 rpm*
MAXIMUM POWER	*6 hp (3 fiscal hp in Italy)*
CYLINDER HEADS AND BARRELS	*separate cast iron barrels, aluminium cylinder heads*
CARBURETTOR	*Dell'Orto UA 15 with filter*
CARBURETTOR DATA	*choke tube 15, coupling M23, valve 55, jet 262, tapered needle C7, 3rd notch, max. jet 60, min. jet 45, toggle 58, float 7.5, inclined float chamber, air intake with filter*
IGNITION	*flywheel magneto with two contact breakers, two sparks per cycle, 6 V 30 W*
CLUTCH	*wet multiplate*
GEARBOX	*unit construction 4-speed constant mesh*
GEAR RATIOS	*1st 26.4, 2nd 16.0, 3rd 10.8, 4th 8.5*

The "Diana" had a completely redesigned yet conventional frame with teledraulic front forks and a rear swinging arm with two shock absorbers. It was cheaper to produce than the "Turismo".

A detail of the motif on the tank of the "Diana" and the headlight fairing with the built-in speedometer.

90

DRIVE	*geared primary, chain secondary*	INSTRUMENTATION	*VDO speedometer calibrated from 1-100 km/h incorporated in the headlight*	
FRAME	*tubular open cradle*	RIDING POSITION	*black leatherette dualseat*	
WHEELBASE	*1315 mm*	FUEL TANK CAPACITY	*14 litres*	
FRONT SUSPENSION	*teledraulic fork*	DRY WEIGHT	*90 kg*	
REAR SUSPENSION	*swinging arm with Standard dampers*	MAXIMUM SPEED	*95 km/h*	
WHEELS	*36 spokes laced onto iron rims*	AVERAGE CONSUMPTION	*33 litres/km*	
TYRES	*2.50 x 19" - front: ribbed; rear: grooved*	LIST PRICE	*180,000 lire ex-works*	
BRAKES	*ø 140 front and rear*	COLOUR RANGE	*red with a black design on the tank and silver pinstriping*	
ELECTRICAL SYSTEM	*Nassetti or Dansi magnetos, ø 130 headlight, rear light*			

A "Diana" with the 175 cm³ engine derived from the 1953 "Gran Turismo"; this version apparently never went into production.

"JUNIOR GENTLEMAN" (1959-1962)

The "Gentleman" was introduced to the Rumi catalogue in 1959, and it was destined to replace the famous "Junior" model in certain markets. Apart from the classic engine, it also inherited the "Junior's" lightweight tubular frame and rear swinging arm. In this particular case, Rumi, for the first time in its admittedly brief motorcycle production history, decided to mount components produced by external specialist companies. The robust telescopic front forks were constructed by Marzocchi, and the dampers and drum brakes were proprietary items available on the market. The rear wheel sprocket was fitted with an anti-snatch device.

The motorcycle was officially introduced to the specialist press in March, 1960. It was intended for Sport class competition and initially it was also offered with a 175 cm^3 engine; the extra cubes were obtained by increasing both the bore and stroke of the 125 cm^3 unit, which obligingly pumped out an extra 6 hp. However, it does not appear that the larger capacity unit was produced in any great number. The "Gentleman" was equipped by the factory with an unusual fuel tank that allowed the mounting of the external magneto already fitted to the sporting models. The lack of demand for this feature later led to the adoption of a simpler fuel tank design. The machine was, of course, supplied with the aluminium alloy cylinders imported from the German K.S. company, but it is by no means rare to find examples of the model fitted with cast iron cylinders. These were undoubtedly used by Rumi just before production ceased. The company also prepared a "Corsa" version reserved for Formula 2 competition, and this machine, fitted with two 22 mm carburettors, made its competition debut in the 125 and 175 cm^3 classes of the 1960 Sassi-Superga classic. Production of the "Gentleman" ended with the closure of the factory.

125 CM³ "GENTLEMAN" (1959-1962)		CARBURETTOR	*Dell'Orto UA 18 Dx-Sx*	The "Gentleman" could be supplied with either twin 18 mm Dell'Ortos sharing a single central float chamber or with racing-type 20 or 22 mm carbs with separate float chambers.
ENGINE	*two-stroke, horizontal parallel twin*	CARBURETTOR DATA	*see 175 cm³ version*	
DISPLACEMENT	*124.68 cm³*	IGNITION	*flywheel magneto with two contact breakers two sparks per cycle, 6 V 30 W*	
BORE AND STROKE	*42 x 45 mm*			
COMPRESSION RATIO	*10.5:1*	CLUTCH	*wet multiplate*	
MAXIMUM RPM	*7,300-8,000 rpm*	GEARBOX	*unit construction 4-speed constant mesh*	
MAXIMUM POWER	*9 hp (3 fiscal hp in Italy)*	GEAR RATIOS	*see 175 cm³ version*	
CYLINDER HEADS AND BARRELS	*in special aluminium, aluminium cylinder heads*	DRIVE	*geared primary, chain secondary, fitted with an anti-snatch device at the rear*	

Two views of the "Gentleman" with the normal tank, which the clientele preferred to the unusual one fitted to the first version. Note that the tank is once more fitted with a chest pad and a small fairing, identical to the one on the "Junior".

94

FRAME	lightweight special steel tubing
WHEELBASE	1275 mm
FRONT SUSPENSION	Marzocchi teledraulic fork
REAR SUSPENSION	swinging arm with Standard dampers
WHEELS	36 spokes laced onto reinforced aluminium rims on iron rims
TYRES	2.50 x 19" - front: ribbed; rear: grooved
BRAKES	front expanding shoe ø 175, rear expanding shoe ø 160
ELECTRICAL SYSTEM	Nassetti or Dansi magnetos, CEV ø 130 headlight, CEV rear light
INSTRUMENTATION	speedometer calibrated from 1-140 km/h incorporated in the headlight
RIDING POSITION	black leather dualseat and pad
FUEL TANK CAPACITY	18 litres - aluminium for the racing bike, iron for the Sport
DRY WEIGHT	87 kg
MAXIMUM SPEED	115 km/h with silencers, 125 km/h with megaphone exhausts
AVERAGE CONSUMPTION	depended on specification
LIST PRICE	200,000 lire ex-works
COLOUR RANGE	see 175 cm³ version.

175 CM³ "GENTLEMAN" (enlarged version)

ENGINE	two-stroke, horizontal twin
DISPLACEMENT	173.75 cm³

It was for the "Gentleman" that Rumi decided to use components built by external specialists for the first time. These included the hydraulically damped telescopic Marzocchi front forks, clearly visible in the photo, along with the faired headlight.

BORE AND STROKE	46 x 52 mm
MAXIMUM POWER	15 hp
CARBURETTOR	Dell'Orto 18 or 22 with separate float chamber
CARBURETTOR DATA	choke tube 18, coupling M23, valve 60, jet 262, tapered needle C1, 2nd notch, max. jet 78, min. jet 45, toggle 58, float 7.5, separate float chamber, racing-type air intake
GEAR RATIOS	1st 24.0, 2nd 17.3, 3rd 12.6, 4th 10.0
MAXIMUM SPEED	150 km/h
COLOUR RANGE	gold with a white design on the tank, red with a white design on the tank, yellow with a yellow design on the tank

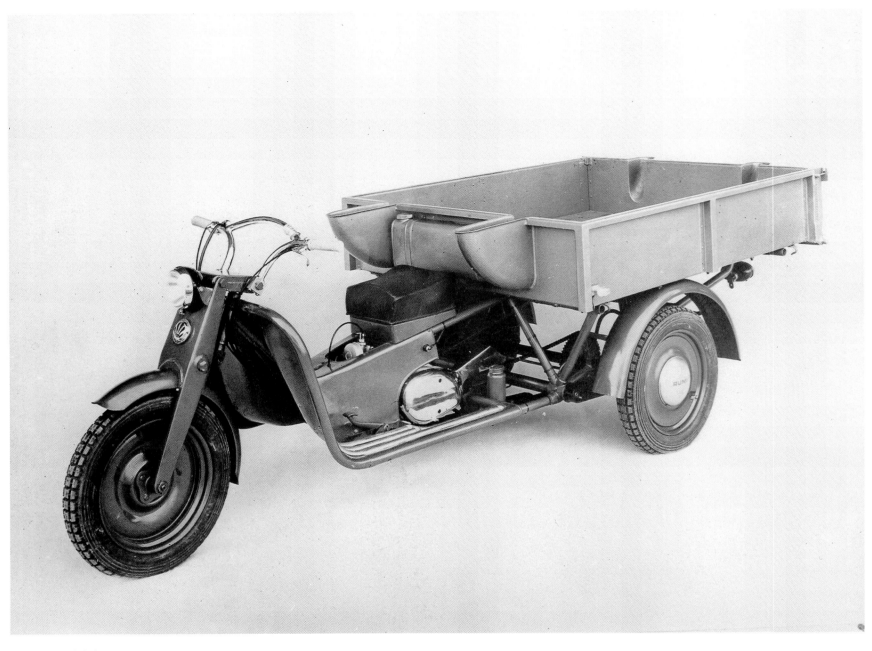

The commercial three-wheeler built between 1950 and 1952 with the 3-speed engine and chain drive.

"125 COMMERCIAL THREE-WHEELER" (1950-1956)

Right from its motorcycling debut, in 1950, Rumi was also involved in commercial vehicle production. The previously mentioned Milan Trade Fair of 1950 also witnessed the introduction of a light delivery tricycle powered by the classic Rumi 125 cm³ twin, mounted in a frame made of bent and welded tubes. A pressed steel parallelogram ruler fork was installed at the front and the engine was located beneath the driver's seat. The mak-

ers claimed a carrying capacity of 300 kg, and it was offered at a list price of 285,000 lire ex-works.

This model, probably put on sale before the completion of an adequate testing programme, proved to be unreliable. A particular problem was the lack of adequate engine ventilation caused by the modest top speed of the vehicle. At the end of 1952, therefore, it was replaced by a new model with decidedly better specifications. The load bearing structure of the vehicle was mixed: the pressed steel front section incorporated the fuel tank

96

Two views of the light commerical three-wheeler, powered by the classic 125 cm³ twin engine and introduced by Rumi in 1950. Having shown itself to be rather unreliable and prone to overheating, this model was replaced in 1952.

On the facing page, the new Rumi "M" type three-wheeler, which remained more or less unchanged until 1956, the year on which production was discontinued. The drive was by shaft and differential and there were two hydraulic drum brakes at the rear. The loading section was made of wood with fibreboard panelling; but a flatbed model with a cabin only was also available.

and was fitted with a traditional telescopic front fork. The rear section, which had to carry the van body, was a tubular structure. The engine with its four speed gearbox was mounted transversally beneath the driver's seat and engine cooling was guaranteed by an efficient forced air system.

The drive was via a propshaft equipped with cardan joints, a live rear axle with fully floating halfshafts that acted as transmission shock absorbers, and a Gleason final drive. The rear wheel braking system, fitted with pedal-operated hydraulic drum brakes, also proved to be very efficient. This commercial vehicle remained practically unchanged throughout its production.

125 CM³ "COMMERCIAL THREE-WHEELER M" (1950-1956)

ENGINE	two-stroke, parallel flat twin, with forced air cooling on the 1952 model
DISPLACEMENT	124.68 cm³
BORE AND STROKE	42 x 45 mm
COMPRESSION RATIO	7.5:1
MAXIMUM RPM	6,000 rpm
MAXIMUM POWER	6 hp (3 fiscal hp in Italy)
CYLINDER HEADS AND BARRELS	separate cast iron, forced-air cooling
CARBURETTOR	Dell'Orto MA 18 B3
CARBURETTOR DATA	choke tube 18, coupling M 26, valve 75, jet 260 B, tapered needle D1, 2nd notch, max. jet 75, min. jet 40, toggle 58, float 6.5, vertical float chamber, air intake with filter
IGNITION	distributor with 6 V 45 W batteries
CLUTCH	multiplate alternating plates in an oil bath
GEARBOX	unit construction 4-speed constant mesh
GEAR RATIOS	unknown
DRIVE	geared primary, shaft secondary with flexible couplings to the differential, Gleason final drive
FRAME	tubes and sheet steel pressings
WHEELBASE AND TRACK	1850 mm, 1040 mm
FRONT SUSPENSION	telescopic fork with return springs
REAR SUSPENSION	coil springs and Standard hydraulic lever dampers
WHEELS	pressed steel
TYRES	front 3.85 x 14", rear 4.25 x 15"
BRAKES	front ø 175 expanding shoe; rear ø 180 pedal-operated hydraulic expanding shoe and handbrake
ELECTRICAL SYSTEM	ø 105 three-lamp CEV headlights, side lights, direction indicators, number plate and stop lamps
INSTRUMENTATION	VDO speedometer calibrated from 1-100 km/h
RIDING POSITION	single saddle
FUEL TANK CAPACITY	12 litres
DRY WEIGHT	200 kg
MAXIMUM SPEED	45 km/h
AVERAGE CONSUMPTION	4.14 litres/100 km
LIST PRICE	301,500 lire ex-works, wooden body 40,000 lire
COLOUR RANGE	Rumi grey with natural wood body, red with natural wood body

The 125 cm³ two-stroke single cylinder engine known as the "Rocket".

GO-KART ENGINES (1960-1966)

There was a remarkable karting boom at the beginning of the Sixties, and a consequence demand for lightweight engines blessed with characteristics such as potent acceleration, ease of maintenance, compact dimensions and cheapness. At that time Rumi was building the "Junior" engine, equipped with aluminium cylinders and twin carburettors, and therefore an involvement in karting seemed a likely source of revenue. At first the company sold individual engine to mechanics and do-it-yourself enthusiasts interested in assembling these original and spartan vehicles. Subsequently Rumi signed a contract - and perhaps had a financial interest in the venture - with the Ital-Kart company (based in Prevalle in the province of Brescia), whereby the kart manufacturer was to supply complete vehicles.

Production got under way with the "Dogi" model, which made its debut on the Rumi stand at the Milan Trade Fair in April, 1960. The frame was made up of varying diameter steel tubing that provided lateral triangulation on both sides. The one-piece driveshaft was rigidly fixed to the chassis via two lateral bushes, and connected to the drive sprocket. The engine was located externally, to the left of the driver's seat, where it enjoyed the most favourable flow of cooling air. A direct steering system was fitted, with the steering wheel operating a small drag link acting on the right-hand wheel, which in turn transmitted the movement to the left-hand wheel via a track rod.

THE "ROCKET" ENGINE

The numerous two-stroke engines of modest cylinder capacities but capable of strong acceleration required by the karting boom of the early Sixties bore a number of prestigious names: Bultaco, Guazzoni, MacCulloch, West-Bend. Rumi also entered the lists in 1960, when it constructed an almost vertical (there was in fact a slight forwards tilt) two-stroke single with a cylinder capacity of 125 cm³ and a unit gearbox. It was clearly inspired by the Spanish school of thought.

The engine was baptized the "Rocket" but engineering and performance details were never released. Production was limited to just a few examples, some of which, mounted in motorcycle frames by amateur motorcycle tuners, finished up participating in Formula Junior competition. At times this led to curious combinations: in 1962, for example, a certain Polenghi took part in the final of the "Trofeo Cadetti" at Monza aboard a hybrid composed of a suitably modified Ducati frame and a single-cylinder Rumi "Rocket" engine.

THE "RS/C" ENGINE

The Rumi company had been closed down for five years when, in 1966, Stefano Rumi, the son of Donnino, bravely attempted a come-back in the kart market. He planned the construction of an original engine to be known as the "RS/C". The crankcase of the engine had been designed so that it could accommodate cylinder capacities of both 125 and 250 cm³.

The "RS/C" was a two-stroke single-cylinder unit (whose "square dimensions of 54 x 54 mm gave it a total capacity of 123.68 cm³) with four-speed unit gearbox and a wet multiplate clutch. The ignition system used a flywheel magneto and was also capable of using the Femsatronik system. The aluminium cylinder featured a cast-iron liner, while special "Dur-Kopp" con-rods were fitted and the gears ran on caged roller bearings. The engine was expected to develop 22 hp at 12500 rpm.

"AMISA" (1949) PROTOTYPE

This prototype represents Rumi's first real experience in motorcycle production and dates back to the period when the company was rapidly pressing in with a partial industrial reconversion programme. The "Amisa" was a kind of mobile test bench, whose primary function was to allow the engine designed by Vassena to be road tested. It was substantially different to the Rumi models produced just two years later.

The name was derived from the initials of the Milan-based specialist firm (A.M.I.S.A.), which produced chassis for light industrial vehicles and various components for motorcycles. This firm

Using the frame built by the Milanese company of the same name, the "Amisa" was fitted with the first Rumi engine designed by Pietro Vassena. When it was first presented (in December 1949) this prototype aroused considerable curiosity and interest.

was commissioned to produce a provisional frame: the result was a conventional closed duplex cradle made of tubular steel, with the engine located at the centre. The suspension system comprised telescopic front forks and a rear swinging arm with a spring box below the crankcase, a layout adopted years earlier by Moto Guzzi. The engine prepared by Rumi had an induction system regulated by a rotating device located between the carburettor and the crankcase, while a twin HT coil fixed below the fuel tank provided current for the spark plugs.

The machine appeared on the A.M.I.S.A. stand at the XXVIIth Cycle and Motorcycle Exhibition at Milan in the December of 1949. It aroused a certain amount of interest in the trade, which was extremely curious to see what the definitive version would look like. Rumi went so far as to indicate an approximate price guide of 200,000 lire, but it does not appear that the machine was ever put into production.

125 CM³ "AMISA" (1949)

ENGINE	*two-stroke, rotary valve twin*
DISPLACEMENT	*not declared*
BORE AND STROKE	*42 x 45 mm*
COMPRESSION RATIO	*not declared*
MAXIMUM RPM	*4,500 rpm*
MAXIMUM POWER	*6 hp*
CYLINDER HEADS AND BARRELS	*separate cast iron*
CARBURETTOR	*Dell'Orto UA 15 in the crankcase*
CARBURETTOR DATA	*see Turismo*
IGNITION	*flywheel magneto with two sparks per cycle*
CLUTCH	*wet multiplate*
GEARBOX	*unit construction 3-speed*
GEAR RATIOS	*not declared*
DRIVE	*geared primary, chain secondary*
FRAME	*duplex cradle*
WHEELBASE AND TRACK	*not declared*
FRONT SUSPENSION	*telescopic fork*
REAR SUSPENSION	*swinging arm with enclosed springs*
WHEELS	*36 spokes laced onto iron rims*
TYRES	*ribbed 2.50 x 18"*
BRAKES	*lateral expanding shoe brakes at front and rear*
ELECTRICAL SYSTEM	*6 V 30 W flywheel magneto, headlight, rear lamp*
INSTRUMENTATION	*not fitted*
RIDING POSITION	*single saddle*
FUEL TANK CAPACITY	*not declared*
DRY WEIGHT	*engine 18 kg, overall weight not declared*
MAXIMUM SPEED	*95 km/h*
AVERAGE CONSUMPTION	*40-50 km/litre*
LIST PRICE	*200,000 lire ex-works*
COLOUR RANGE	*metallic silver*

"GRAND PRIX" (1952) PROTOTYPE

Rumi's desire to participate in topflight motorcycle competition took concrete form in 1952 when a 250 Grand Prix machine was designed and built by Salmaggi, considered a wizard with four-stroke engines.

The engine - a parallel twin with the cylinders slightly tilted forwards and double overhead camshafts driven by a central gear train - was considered by some experts to be a derivative of the famous four-cylinder Gilera unit, which Salmaggi had helped to prepare. The machine's first outing was at Monza in April 1952 in front of a large crowd of observers, including Donnino Rumi of course. The rider upon whose shoulders the responsibility for this first public exhibition rested was Bruno Romano, who had already performed brilliantly in races and trials events with the 125s. The machine, which boasted simple but undeniably elegant looks, had been constructed using refined technology. It featured a duplex cradle frame with leading link front forks, whilst the rear swinging arm was equipped with vertical hydraulically damped telescopic suspension struts.

The general appearance of the machine resembled a scaled-up version of the excellent "Gobbetto" - it had the same extended fuel tank projecting beyond the steering head with sculpted sides to accommodate the rider's arms. At a later date, i.e. when the Grand Prix Rumi made its appearance in late autumn at the Milan Cycle and Motorcycle Show, the tank appeared in its definitive from with a two-tone colour scheme.

No precise details were provided regarding the engine, and nothing is known as to why the project was abandoned after it had aroused the approval of the press from the very beginning. It is conceivable that those first road tests - timed manually - did not satisfy the engineers and that it was not deemed possible to make the machine competitive. In that period the 250 class was dominated by the Moto Guzzi "Gambalunghino", with only the rejuvenated Benelli providing any effective competition, though towards the end of the international season the NSU "Rennmax" twin was already making a considerable impact. In 1952 both the Guzzi and the NSU were already capable of reaching top speeds of over 180 km/h, and could lap Monza at averages of 153-154 km/h. The elegant new Rumi was probably unable to match these figures.

A side view of the "Grand Prix" 250, built in 1951 by Luigi Salmaggi, one of the great designers of the fast 4-stroke engines. Rumi had this model built with a view to making a name for itself in high level contemporary competition.

103

A three-quarters view of the "Grand Prix". The man who rode this model on its first public appearances at the Monza Autodrome in the April of 1952 was Bruno Romano.

250 CM³ "GRAND PRIX" (1952)

ENGINE	*four-stroke, parallel twin, dohc*
DISPLACEMENT	*250 cm³*
BORE AND STROKE	*not declared*
COMPRESSION RATIO	*not declared*
MAXIMUM RPM	*not declared*
MAXIMUM POWER	*not declared*
CYLINDER HEADS AND BARRELS	*inclined forwards ay 27°, separate castings*
CARBURETTOR	*twin-barrel Dell'Orto with separate float chamber*
CARBURETTOR DATA	*not declared*
IGNITION	*magneto*
LUBRICATION	*gear-type feed pump, gravity return; wet sump*
CLUTCH	*in oil bath*
GEARBOX	*4 speeds in unit*

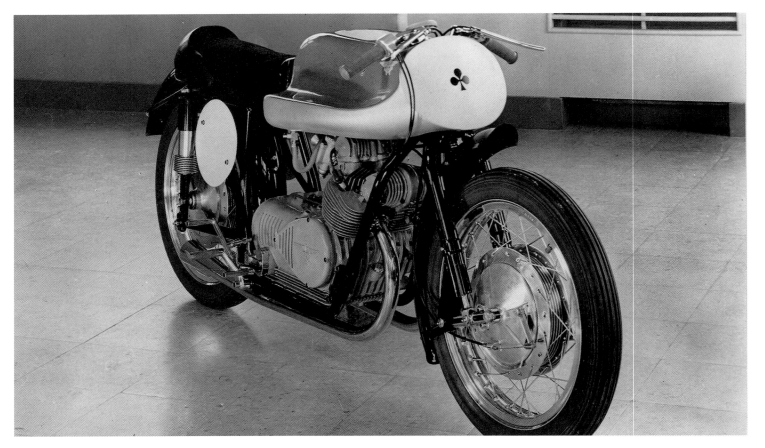

Despite the initial enthusiasm, the "Grand Prix" project never got off the ground. In all probability this was due to poor results during testing, which revealed that the bike's performance was well below that of rival machinery involved in the World Championship.

105

Some details of the "Grand Prix": left, the cardan shaft, the brake drum and the swinging arm rear suspension with the upright hydraulic suspension units; right, the dohc parallel twin engine with the pots tilted slightly forward was considered by experts to be a derivation of the famous Gilera four.

GEAR RATIOS	*not declared*
DRIVE	*geared primary, cardan shaft secondary with constant velocity joints*
FRAME	*lightweight tubular open duplex cradle*
WHEELBASE	*not declared*
FRONT SUSPENSION	*leading links, return springs*
REAR SUSPENSION	*swinging arm with vertical hydraulic dampers*
WHEELS	*spokes laced onto 19" aluminium rims*
TYRES	*front: ribbed 3.00 x 19"; rear: grooved*
BRAKES	*front: expanding twin-shoe type; rear: central expanding type*

ELECTRICAL SYSTEM	*not declared*
INSTRUMENTATION	*rev-counter incorporated in the fuel tank*
RIDING POSITION	*racing type*
FUEL TANK CAPACITY	*not declared*
DRY WEIGHT	*not declared*
MAXIMUM SPEED	*not declared*
AVERAGE CONSUMPTION	*not declared*
LIST PRICE	*not declared*
COLOUR RANGE	*black, tank in red and ivory*

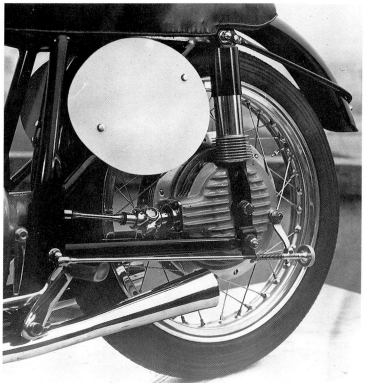

"BIALBERO" (1953) PROTOTYPE

The "Bialbero" ("twin-cam") constitutes an authentic novelty for the enthusiasts as it was never officially presented or exhibited at any show or exhibition. Presumably, the marque's intention was to enter Grand Prix competition with a view to conquering the 125 title, but it should be remembered that at that time, this class was dominated by the MV Agusta twin-cam, the NSU "Rennfox", the Mondial twin-cam and the Morini single-cam, all of them four-stroke singles.

The prototype of this bike was designed and constructed between 1952 and 1953, when Luigi Salmaggi was still working at Rumi and, judging by the architecture of the engine, it would seem logical to attribute the project to him. The engine underwent lengthy trials on the test bench, but it is not known whether it was ever tested on the road. What we do know, however, thanks to the photographic evidence that has been put together, is how it was conceived. The frame used - presumably on a temporary basis - was taken from the MkII "Gobbetto" and, looking at it now, it seems clearly out of proportion to the bulky dimensions of the engine, and inadequate to cope with the power that the latter would have been able to provide.

The prototype "Bialbero" (twin-cam) designed between 1952 and 1953. The frame used, probably on a provisional basis since it is dwarfed by the voluminous engine, was that of the second series "Gobbetto". The "Bialbero" engine is here shown during bench-testing.

125 CM³ "BIALBERO" (1953)

ENGINE	*four-stroke single, shaft-and-bevel-driven twin cams; separate lubrication*
DISPLACEMENT	*125 cm³*
BORE AND STROKE	*not declared*
COMPRESSION RATIO	*not declared*
MAXIMUM RPM	*not declared*
MAXIMUM POWER	*not declared*
CYLINDER HEADS AND BARRELS	*in special aluminium*
CARBURETTOR	*Dell'Orto 26 mm*
CARBURETTOR DATA	*not declared*
IGNITION	*magneto*
CLUTCH	*wet-plate*
GEARBOX	*4 speeds*
GEAR RATIOS	*not declared*
DRIVE	*geared primary, chain secondary*
FRAME	*lightweight tubular open cradle*
WHEELBASE	*not declared*
FRONT SUSPENSION	*leading links*
REAR SUSPENSION	*swinging arm with lateral dampers*
WHEELS	*spokes laced onto aluminium rims*
TYRES	*front: ribbed 2.00 x 18"; rear: 2.50 x 17"*
BRAKES	*front: twin-shoe, central expansion brake; rear: central expansion brake*
ELECTRICAL SYSTEM	*Dansi flywheel magneto*
INSTRUMENTATION	*rev-counter on the fuel tank*
RIDING POSITION	*racing type single saddle*
FUEL TANK CAPACITY	*22 litres (aluminium)*
DRY WEIGHT	*not declared*
MAXIMUM SPEED	*not declared*
AVERAGE CONSUMPTION	*not declared*
LIST PRICE	*not declared*
COLOUR RANGE	*black, red*

Left on the facing page, two views of the engine fitted to the "Bialbero" prototype. Considering the period in which the bike was built and the basic architecture of the engine, the project seems almost certainly the work of Ing. Salmaggi.

"V.T. - VALVOLE IN TESTA" (1954) PROTOTYPE

The demands of the market were changing, as bike buyers leaned progressively towards more sophisticated and more powerful vehicles. These conditions encouraged Rumi to design and construct a four-stroke light-middleweight that seemed assured of an interesting niche in the market. The project was the work of Bruno Guidorossi, whose design was presented in prototype form at the Cycle and Motorcycle Show at the end of 1955.

Guidorossi's precise engineering specified intake and exhaust valves at an included angle of 36°, domed pistons, a 120 mm connecting rod, a 27 mm diameter exhaust manifold and a clutch with seven alternating plates.

Alongside the "Turismo" model, "Sport" and "Supersport" versions were also planned. These differed from the base model only in terms of the compression ratio and the type of carburation. For example, the "Supersport" model was designed to run on a 9.5:1 compression ratio using a carburettor with a 25 mm choke tube.

The "V.T." ("ohv" in Italian) was an extremely attractive bike; a single colour scheme was offered: red with black or white pinstriping on the fuel tank. Performance was respectable with a maximum power output of 10 hp and a top speed of 115 km/h. One has to presume that development of the project foundered on the rock of Rumi's lack of technical experience in the four-stroke field. The 175 "V.T." never progressed beyond the prototype stage.

175 CM³ "V.T." (1954)	
ENGINE	four-stroke oh valve (pushrods and rockers), single cylinders inclined forwards at 12°, pressure lubrication
DISPLACEMENT	173.60 cm³
BORE AND STROKE	62 x 57.5 mm
COMPRESSION RATIO	7:1
MAXIMUM RPM	6700 rpm
MAXIMUM POWER	10 hp
CYLINDER HEADS AND BARRELS	aluminium

A nice shot of the 175 cm³ "V.T." project, powered by a middleweight 4-stroke engine. In building this model, designed by Guidorossi in 1954, Rumi clearly wished to tap the growing interest in faster, more powerful bikes. The fact that this project was shelved was due to Rumi's lack of specialist 4-stroke engineering know-how.

A three-quarters view of the "175 V.T.".

CARBURETTOR	*22 mm Dell'Orto with 29 mm induction tract*
CARBURETTOR DATA	*not declared*

FOTO WELLS - BERGAMO

IGNITION	*Marelli magneto with automatic advance*
CLUTCH	*wet multiplate*
GEARBOX	*4-speed unit construction with heel and toe rocking pedal*
GEAR RATIOS	*not declared*
DRIVE	*helical gear primary, chain secondary*
FRAME	*tubular open cradle, suspended engine*
WHEELBASE	*not declared*
FRONT SUSPENSION	*teledraulic fork*
REAR SUSPENSION	*swinging arm with hydraulic dampers*
WHEELS	*spokes laced onto aluminium rims*
TYRES	*2.50 x 19" reinforced*
BRAKES	*rear central expanding shoe brakes at front and rear*
ELECTRICAL SYSTEM	*Marelli dynamo 45 W 6 V, ø 130 3 lamp headlight, 9 ah battery*
INSTRUMENTATION	*speedometer incorporated in the headlight*
RIDING POSITION	*leatherette dualseat*
FUEL TANK CAPACITY	*16 litres*
DRY WEIGHT	*115 kg*
MAXIMUM SPEED	*115 km/h, max. gradient 25%*
AVERAGE CONSUMPTION	*40 km/litre*
LIST PRICE	*not declared*
COLOUR RANGE	*red with a black design on the fuel tank*

"BICILINDRICA 4 TEMPI ROLLA" (1954) PROTOTYPE

Visitors to the Rumi stand at the 1954 Cycle and Motorcycle Exhibition were electrified by the sight of a Grand Prix motorcycle boasting some fairly unusual specifications. The machine in question was a four-stroke flat twin with twin overhead camshafts actuated by gears on the left-hand side of the engine and a cylinder capacity of 125 cm³. The engine was clearly derived from the well known two-stroke unit, whilst the frame was the same as that of the second series "Gobbetto".

It was in fact a well thought out conversion job based on the two-stroke engine used in the Rumi racing machines. The author of this conversion was, without any shadow of a doubt, an enthusiast from La Spezia called Felice Rolla, who was well known in motorcycling circles as an expert racing bike tuner. It is probable that Rumi as a company, and perhaps Guidorossi in person, approached this expert craftsman with an offer to help out with the bench testing and tuning of the new engine. Even though it was not directly constructed by the company, it was thought right to include this "special" in the chapter dedicated to the prototypes as, at the time, it was publicized as a Rumi product and its omission might have caused some readers to suspect an unforgivable lapse.

The "Rolla" twin was named after its creator, a well known and gifted competition bike preparer, and was introduced in December 1954. It used the rear swinging arm from the "Gobbetto" and a Marelli external magneto.

125 CM³ "BICILINDRICA 4 T. ROLLA" (1954)

ENGINE	four-stroke twin, twin camshafts actuated by a gear train
DISPLACEMENT	124.68 cm³
BORE AND STROKE	not declared
COMPRESSION RATIO	not declared
MAXIMUM RPM	not declared
MAXIMUM POWER	not declared
CYLINDER HEADS AND BARRELS	separate aluminium cylinders, aluminium heads
CARBURETTOR	Dell'Orto SS1 22C
CARBURETTOR DATA	choke tube 22, coupling M 25.4, valve 70, jet 265, tapered needle R2, 3rd notch, max. jet 115, min.jet 50, float 11, float chamber SS2, bellmouth air intake
IGNITION	twin spark Bosch UZ/IF 2L1 magneto
CLUTCH	wet multiplate
GEARBOX	4-speed constant mesh
GEAR RATIOS	not declared
DRIVE	geared primary, chain secondary
FRAME	open cradle in special lightweight tubing
WHEELBASE	not declared
FRONT SUSPENSION	leading link
REAR SUSPENSION	s/arm with shock absorbers
WHEELS	36 spokes laced onto aluminium rims, front 18", rear 17"
TYRES	front: ribbed 2.00 x 18"; rear: grooved 2.50 x 17"
BRAKES	front: central twin-shoe drum; rear: central drum
ELECTRICAL SYSTEM	external Marelli magneto
INSTRUMENTATION	rev counter
RIDING POSITION	black leather racing saddle
FUEL TANK CAPACITY	22 litres (aluminium)
DRY WEIGHT	88 kg
MAXIMUM SPEED	not declared
AVERAGE CONSUMPTION	not declared
LIST PRICE	not declared
COLOUR RANGE	ivory with a yellow design on the fuel tank

On the facing page, a close up of the 4-stroke 2-cylinder "Rolla" engine. The twin cams were driven by a gear train on the left hand side of the engine. In the photo below the Guzzi-derived scavenge pump can clearly be seen to the left of the flywheel.

V1 STRADA (1960) PROTOTYPE

This was in all probability the most original project, at least as far as the mechanical side was concerned, ever conceived by Rumi's engineering division. It appeared in April 1960 on the Bergamo based company's stand at the Milan Trade Fair, where the engine in particular aroused considerable attention. It was a very compact, longitudinal, four-stroke V-twin with horizontal finning. The design was the work of Umberto Ottolenghi.

During the design phase of this very well balanced twin, particular attention was paid to the cooling of the rear cylinder, notoriously less exposed to the air flow in this particular layout. The designer thought to solve the problem by offsetting the cylinders by 8 mm, so that the second cylinder would also benefit from the dynamic air flow. Both cylinders were cooled by ranks of horizontal parallel fins.

According to the criteria that Rumi was gradually adopting, this engine was to have powered both a motorcycle and a brand new scooter. Plans were made to produce the engine with various cylinder capacities: 98 cm³ (compression ratio 8.4:1, 5.8 hp at

7500 rpm); 125 cm³ (compression ratio 8:1, 6.8 hp at 7000 rpm); and lastly 175 cm³ (compression ratio 8:1, 8.2 hp at 6800 rpm).
The motorcycle that the Milanese public had a chance to admire certainly lived up to Rumi's name for innovation, original mechanical design, attractive styling and well chose colour schemes. Unfortunately, the motorcycle and the scooter with the longitudinal V-twin engine appeared at a time when Rumi company already sliding into decline, and they both remained as prototypes.

125 CM³ "V1 STRADA" (1960)	
ENGINE	four-stroke 90° V twin; lubrication via a geared pump
DISPLACEMENT	124.82 cm³
BORE AND STROKE	43 x 43 mm
COMPRESSION RATIO	8:1
MAXIMUM RPM	7000 rpm

The prototype of the "125 V1 Strada" was shown at the 1960 Milan Trade Fair. Visitors to the show liked the design of the new mechanicals, the colour schemes, and the bike's looks in general.

MAXIMUM POWER	6.8 hp		FRAME	lightweight tubular open cradle
CYLINDER HEADS AND BARRELS	separate with overhead valves and pushrods and rockets		WHEELBASE	not declared
CARBURETTOR	16 mm Dell'Orto with dual inlet manifold		FRONT SUSPENSION	teledraulic fork
CARBURETTOR DATA	not declared		REAR SUSPENSION	swinging arm with hydraulic dampers
IGNITION	flywheel magneto		WHEELS	36 spokes laced onto steel rims
CLUTCH	wet multiplate		TYRES	2.50 x 18" - front: ribbed; rear: grooved
GEARBOX	unit construction 4-speed constant mesh with heel and toe rocking pedal		BRAKES	front ø 175 expanding shoe, rear ø 160 expanding shoe
			ELECTRICAL SYSTEM	Dansi magneto, ø 130 3 lamp CEV headlight, ø 70 rear light
GEAR RATIOS	not declared		INSTRUMENTATION	VDO speedometer calibrated from 1-120 km/h incorporated in the headlight
DRIVE	geared primary, chain secondary with anti-snatch device		RIDING POSITION	suede dualseat

The "125 V1 Strada", shown here in the "Sport" version, was equipped with an extremely compact 4-stroke longitudinal vee-twin engine with horizontal finning designed by Umberto Ottolenghi.

FUEL TANK CAPACITY	*14 litres (iron)*
DRY WEIGHT	*85 kg*
MAXIMUM SPEED	*105 km/h*
AVERAGE CONSUMPTION	*40 km/litre*
LIST PRICE	*150,000 lire ex-works*
COLOUR RANGE	*silver with an ivory design on the fuel tank and gold pinstriping, red with a white design on the fuel tank*

A detail of the "Strada"s vee-twin engine; versions of this unit with various capacities were planned both for the lightweight motorcycle and an original scooter.

Right, a partial view of the teledraulic front fork and the central drum brake with the cooling slits. On the facing page, the "Turismo 125" version of the "V1 Strada". Unfortunately both the "Strada" and the scooter, both fitted with the longitudinal V engine, never got beyond the prototype stage.

"V1 MOTOSCOOTER" (1960) PROTOTYPE

This was the scooter version, with small wheels and enclosed bodywork, of the motorcycle described above, alongside which it was presented to the public in April 1960, also with planned cylinder capacities of 98, 125 and 175 cm³. One note of technical interest here was the forced air ventilation system on the right-hand, i.e. exhaust side of the engine. This ensured that the cylinders were cooled properly despite the bodywork. The styling of the scooter, even though it was not wholly original, was attractive enough with pleasingly fluid lines, whilst the chassis was completed by a two-tone dualseat. Only a few prototypes of the "V1" scooter were produced.

125 CM³ "V1" MOTOSCOOTER (1960)	
ENGINE	four-stroke 90° V-twin; lubrication via a geared pump
DISPLACEMENT	124.82 cm³
BORE AND STROKE	43 x 43 mm
COMPRESSION RATIO	8:1
MAXIMUM RPM	7,000 rpm
MAXIMUM POWER	6.8
CYLINDER HEADS AND BARRELS	separate, vee configuration, ohv, pushrods and rockers, forced air cooling
CARBURETTOR	16 mm Dell'Orto with dual inlet manifold
CARBURETTOR DATA	not declared
IGNITION	flywheel magneto
CLUTCH	wet multiplate
GEARBOX	unit construction 4-speed constant mesh
GEAR RATIOS	not declared

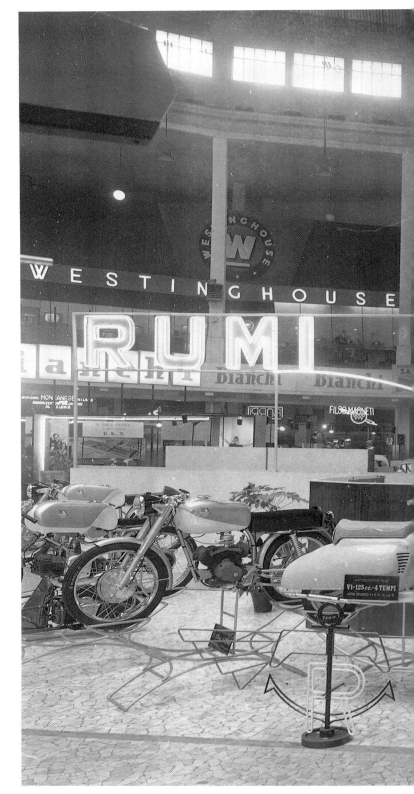

The "V1 Motoscooter" at the Milan Trade Fair in the April of 1960.

124

DRIVE	*geared primary, chain secondary*
FRAME	*pressed steel monocoque*
WHEELBASE	*not declared*
FRONT SUSPENSION	*leading links and damper springs*
REAR SUSPENSION	*swinging arm and damper rings*
WHEELS	*interchangeable pressed steel type*
TYRES	*3.50 x 10"*
BRAKES	*front and rear ø 125 expanding shoe*
ELECTRICAL SYSTEM	*Dansi magneto, cantilevered headlight on the handlebar*
INSTRUMENTATION	*not fitted*
RIDING POSITION	*leatherette dualseat*
FUEL TANK CAPACITY	*not declared*
DRY WEIGHT	*not declared*
MAXIMUM SPEED	*98 km/h*
AVERAGE CONSUMPTION	*not declared*
LIST PRICE	*125,000 lire ex-works*
COLOUR RANGE	*Rumi grey*

The 4-stroke "V1 Moto-scooter". On the right hand side of the engine there was an interesting forced ventilation system that ensured perfect cylinder cooling. This bike's flowing lines were graceful and pleasing.

RUMI
PORTFOLIO

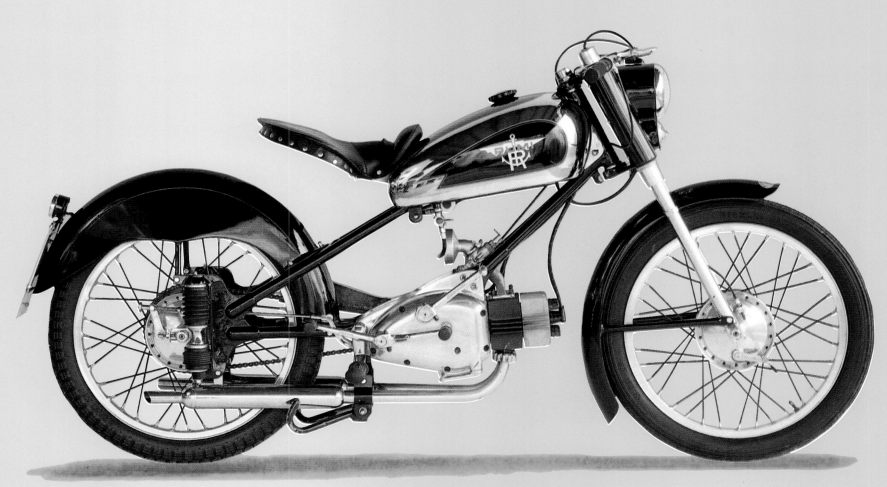

A model from 1950
Collection Giovanni De Marchi - ASI no. 1792

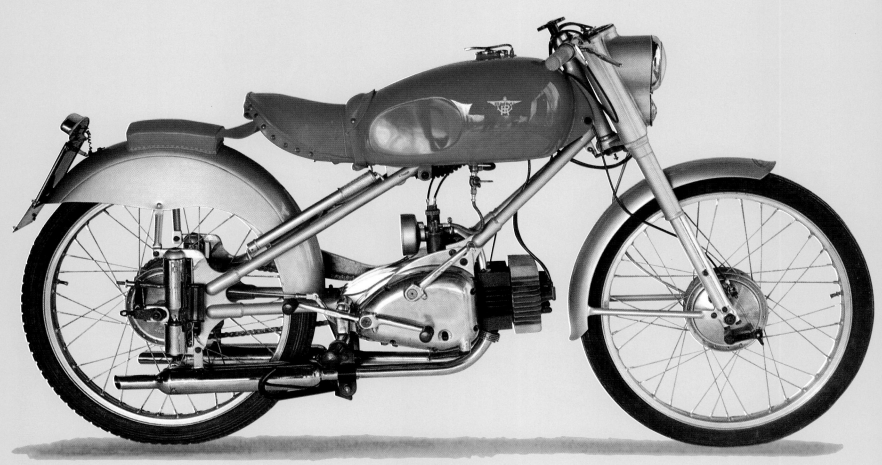

A model from 1952
Private collection - ASI no. 1128

Competition SS 52 1ª serie
125 cm³

A model from 1952
Collection Ferruccio Maroli

A model from 1955
Original period photograph

Formichino
125 cm³

A model from 1955
Collection Giuseppe Pullici

-Bicarburatore Esportazione-
125 cm³

A model from 1955
Original period photograph

Bicarburatore SS
125 cm³

A model from 1954
Private collection - ASI no. 1062

GT Granturismo
200 cm³

A model from 1956
Original period photograph

Turismo 3 velocità 125 cm³

A model from 1953
Collection Giovanni De Marchi - ASI no. 1791

Regolarità Sei Giorni 125 cm³

A model from 1955
Collection Stefano Rumi

A model from 1952
Collection Aquilino Scarpellini - ASI no. 1261

Junior Earles Esportazione 125 cm³

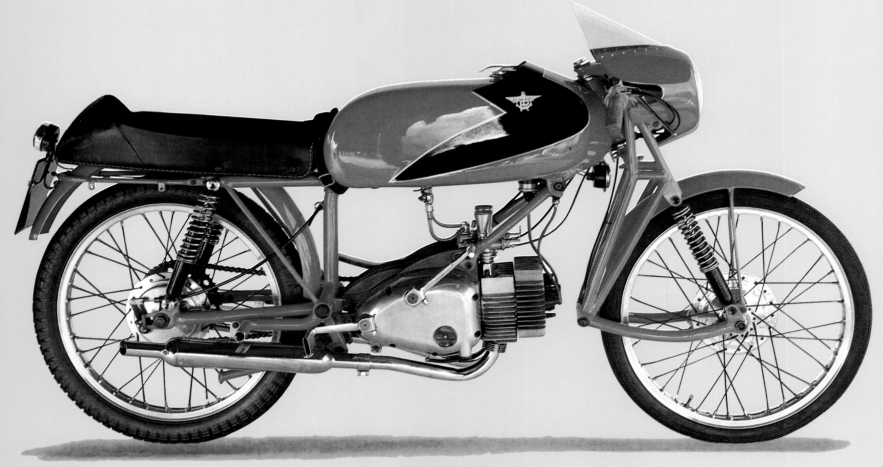

A model from 1956
Collection Gösta Karlsson

Junior Telescopico
125 cm³

A model from 1959
Private collection - ASI no. 1125

Diana
125 cm³

Model from 1956
Original period photograph

Junior Gentleman
125 cm³

Model from 1962
Private collection

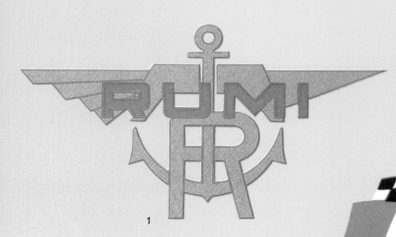

Rumi 200cc

Rumi

1. The tank badging used on the first models produced in 1950 and at the beginning of 1951. 2. The Rumi firm's trade mark was also used as an emblem for the marque's motorcycles. 3. The emblem adopted by Rumi for its competition bikes from 1995, following the marque's victory in two classes of the Italian speed championship. 4. The logo applied to the centre of the fuel tank on the 175 and 200 cm³ versions of the "G.T.- Granturismo". 5. The badge indicating the cubic capacity, which was mounted on the mudguard fin of the "Granturismo". 6. The screenprinted badging use as an alternative to the tank logo on the "Granturismo". 7. The first identification plate used by dealers and authorized garages. 8. The second such identification plate.

HONOUR ROLL
1950-1961

Note

The following pages, dedicated to the results notched up by Rumi in little more than a decade spent in the sporting arena, obviously are not - nor can they be expected to be - exhaustive. Rumi, a favourite with privateers, was simply present at too many events. Nevertheless, the following pages give a considerably full - if not wholly comprehensive - picture of the Bergamo-based manufacturer's presence on the sporting scene and the degree of success it enjoyed.

The races, arranged in paragraphs year by year, are in chronological order. For each event we have given all the data it was possible to find, such as the race numbers, the name and surname of the competitor and the rankings. Unless specified otherwise, it should be understood that the competition class was that reserved for 125 cm^3 machines.

A SPORTING VOCATION

RUMI AND COMPETITION

The beginning of Rumi's competition career was more or less contemporaneous with the launch of the first standard production models. Three months after the presentation of its brand new motorcycle at the Milan Trade Fair, Rumi fielded two of its machines at the Trofeo Orobico, a trials event held in Bergamo in July 1950.

The company's brief competition history, which spanned the years between 1950 and 1962, certainly cannot be compared to that of other marques actively involved in racing at the time, but it nevertheless had a character of its own and remains worthy of note. Rumi's competition models were prepared for participation in trials or speed events, both on the track and on the road. They were all powered by tweaked versions of the normal production engines mounted on the standard "over the counter" models. Slightly modifications were made to the carburation, the exhaust system and the transmission, and more specifically, the final drive ratios.

Only in a few rare cases were Rumi competition bikes radically different from the standard road-going models and therefore unsuitable for normal use. In this case, the outstanding example was the celebrated "Gobbetto", which boasted an unusual fuel tank extended forward of the steering head whence it was abruptly sliced off, similar the one seen on the Moto Guzzi Grand Prix 500 twin of a few years earlier.

The particular qualities of these small yet sparkling 125s fuelled the aspirations of numerous young, would-be champions, who had plenty of enthusiasm but little in the way of financial resources. Thanks to the affordable little Rumi these youngsters could get a ride in 2nd and 3rd category competition with a real chance of obtaining the success that would otherwise have been denied them. For its part, Rumi saw involvement in competition as an incentive to commercial development and the diffusion of its model on the market. The company therefore approved of sporting activities, particularly in the period 1952-1955, when it fielded a works team.

The Bergamo-based marque's racing division was organized by Luigi Salmaggi with the help of his right-hand mechanic Orlando Ciceroni, whom we mentioned earlier. At first the riders were "discovered" and selected from among the numerous testers employed by Rumi, some of whom revealed considerable, if unexpected, racing talent. In competition, the Rumi 125s found themselves up against the technical superiority of the aristocratic four-stroke racing bikes of the period: the single-cam Morini, the Mondial and the twin-cam MV Agusta, all purpose-built for topflight speed events. Their superiority was particularly apparent on high-speed tracks and one example serves to illustrate the problem faced by Rumi: at Monza in 1952, the Rumi was capable of lapping at an average speed of 120 km/h whilst the fastest lap during that year's Grand Prix of Nations was recorded by the MV Agusta at 138 km/h. Nevertheless, on circuits where acceleration and lightness, combined with the skill of the rider, played a greater part, the Rumi was often unrivalled. In fact the marque's greatest successes were notched up in hillclimb events - where they often set new records - or on urban, round-the-houses circuits. In these categories the Rumi riders won a number of Italian national riders' titles, whilst the team obtained respectable placings in the constructors' championships. The Rumi twins also distinguished themselves on a number of occasions in long distance or endurance events such as the Milano-Taranto, the Motorcycling Giro d'Italia, and the Liège-Milan-Liège. The Rumi's unexpected reliability and stamina over long distances aroused considerable surprise among both experts and enthusiasts alike; on more than one occasion that surprise verged on incredulity as the Rumis defeated what were, on paper, far superior machines with much greater cylinder capacities.

The Milano-Taranto event, an immensely long gallop from the North to the extreme South of the peninsula, is a case in point. In the 1952 event, Bruno Romano from Casale obtained third place at an average speed of 85.239 km/h, and actually won the 125 Competition class two years later at an average speed of 91.454 km/h. In the 1953 Motorcycling Giro d'Italia the machines ridden by Luigi Ciai, Roberto Vigorito and Bruno Romano were placed second, third and fourth respectively.

The speciality best suited to the characteristics of the Rumi motorcycle and the competitive spirit of its riders was undoubtedly the tough and testing world of trials competitions. Bergamo boasted a lively trials tradition, on the one hand for the "Valli Bergamasche" and the various other important trophy competitions traditionally held in the area, and on the other for the parallel flowering in local sporting circles of an extremely high quality school of expert trials riders, without doubt the best in Italy. In this field Rumi obtained numerous successes (as can be seen from the roll of honour accompanying these

147

Achille Rumi, Donnino's son, tackles a hill during Bergamo's Circuito delle Mura event. Between 1951 and 1952 Achille Rumi took part in both trials and speed events as a member of the Rumi works team.

pages), of which the marque was always particularly proud. The apotheosis was reached at the end of the International Six Day event, held in 1954 at Llandrindod Wells in Great Britain. Here the riders of the four Rumi machines entered - Dario Basso, Pietro Carissoni, Miro Riva and Bruno Romano - were all awarded gold medals. In that edition of the classic international trials event the only other Italians to win gold medals were Fenocchio, Serafini and Saini on Gileras, Daminelli on a Mi-Val, and Fornasari on an MV Agusta.

But the "Formichino" (the "Little Ant") was ignored by Italian enthusiasts, even though scooter racing had become so popular that an official national championship was established in the early Fifties. In its various versions, however, it became a veritable standby for the French and Belgian specialists in the exhausting "24 Hours" race held at Monthléry, where it did very well and never failed to improve on the average chalked up in the preceding races. In the Rumi roll of honour, special mention should be made of the Italian origins of the multiple victories obtained by the Italo-Venezuelan Ferruccio Dalle Fusine, three times national champion.

During our research into Rumi's sporting victories, we repeatedly asked ourselves whether it would be appropriate to record only the victories of the various riders, or whether we ought to include placings or even entry lists in general. By and large, Rumi's sporting history is the story of the enthusiasm, the disinterested participation, and the spirit of sacrifice of a host of genuine enthusiasts who, through ill-luck or lack of economic means, never enjoyed the thrill of outright victory. And so, since we believe in the Olympic spirit and the notion that taking part is more important that winning, we felt it was only right to include everybody. A small repayment for their enthusiastic and generous dedication to that marvellous motorcycle, the Rumi.

Ferruccio Delle Fusine during a Venezuelan National Championship event in 1955. He is riding a Rumi 125 with a characteristic aluminium "bird beak" fairing.

At Bergamo's Trofeo Orobico of the 23rd July 1950: from left to right, no. 58 Angelo Troisi, no. 56 Pietro Bignoli, and no. 57 Gianni Zonca.

1950

LEONESSA DI BRESCIA - Trials event
16.7.1950

Angelo Troisi	2nd
Rino Prati	8th

TROFEO OROBICO - Bergamo - Trials event
23.7.1950

Pietro Brignoli	12th
Gianni Zonca	15th
Angelo Troisi	18th

VERMICINO-ROCCA DI PAPA
October 1950

Carlini	3rd

150

The first Giro di Sicilia was held between the 13th and 15th of October 1950: the photo shows Gianni Zonca, astride an all-new Rumi "Sport", at a check point.

The first speed event won by Rumi, thanks to the skills of Angelo Troisi (in the photo on the right), was the Circuito del Cidneo of the 1st November 1950. Note the competition specification of the production "Sport", with a slightly faired front mudguard, no lights and long megaphone exhausts.

1st GIRO MOTOCICLISTICO DI SICILIA
Palermo - Trials event
13/15.10.1950

Angelo Troisi	1st
Gianni Zonca	1st
Pietro Brignoli	1st

Team	1st

CIRCUITO DEL CIDNEO - Brescia - Speed event
1.11.1950

16 Angelo Troisi	1st

CITTÀ DI GENOVA - Tourist Board - Trials event
4.11.1950

Angelo Troisi	1st
Domenico Cavalli	1st
Pietro Brignoli	1st
Gianni Zonca	1st

The City of Genoa Trophy, 4th of November 1950: from left to right we can recognize Pietro Brignoli, Adriano Chiabrera (the Rumi agent for Genoa), Donnino Rumi, Gianni Zonca, Achille Rumi and Angelo Troisi.

153

The first works team at the 6th edition of the Primi Passi event, in April 1951. From left to right, Guerino Mantovani, Angelo Troisi, Pietro Brignoli, Domenico Cavalli, and Gianni Zonca. The two bikes in the foreground are "Sports"; note the Zonca's carburettor is fitted with individual float chambers.

1951

CITTÀ DI TRAPANI - Trials event
4.3.1951

Pietro Lombardo	1st

TROFEO ALDRIGHETTI - Milano
March 1951

Franco Ubbiali	10th
Angelo Troisi	10th

Pietro Brignoli	10th
Ovidio Agosti	22nd
Nino Presenti	25th
Molinari	28th

TRE VALLI VARESINE - Trials event
19.3.1951

Guerino Mantovani	1st
Angelo Troisi	1st
Nino Presenti	1st
Otello Spadoni	1st
Molinari	1st

Gianni Zonca	1st
Ovidio Agosti	1st
Pietro Brignoli	1st

COPPA SPAGGIANI - Parma - Trials event
18.3.1951

Ennio Gandolfi	1st
Guido Gavazzini	1st
Domenico Giusto	1st
Angelo Raimondo	1st

6th PRIMI PASSI - Trials event
April 1951

36 Gianni Zonca	1st
Guerino Mantovani	1st
Angelo Troisi	1st

2nd COPPA CITTÀ DI GENOVA - Provincial trials event
15.4.1951

| Canducci | 7th |

5th TROFEO DEI LAGHI - Provincial trials event
25.4.1951

Angelo Troisi	1st
Pietro Brignoli	1st
Guglielmo Strada	1st
Gianni Zonca	1st
Guerino Mantovani	1st
Onorato Francone	42nd

COPPA MALADOSA - Bergamo - Provincial trials event
3.5.1951

| G. Mario Paleari | 1st |

| Pietro Cassironi | 13th |
| Achille Rumi | 14th |

SALITA DELLE TORRICELLE - Verona - Hillclimb
May 1951

| Gianni Zonca | 1st |

3rd SCUDO DEL SUD - Foggia - Trials event
10.5.1951

Angelo Troisi	18th
Onorato Francone	26th
Guerino Mantovani	28th

GIRO DELL'UMBRIA - Trials event
27.5.1951

| Marino Faina | 5th |

A snap (dated 3rd of May 1951) taken during the Coppa Maladosa, a trials event held over the Presolana Pass, near Bergamo. Between the two motorcycles, in overalls, is Achille Rumi, who came 14th in the race; standing on his left are his younger brother Stefano and his father Donnino.

155

COPPA LEONESSA - Brescia - National trials event
3.6.1951

Angelo Troisi	1st
Achille Rumi	1st
Guerino Mantovani	1st
Rino Prati	1st
Gianni Zonca	1st
Onorato Francone	1st
Pietro Carissoni	1st

COLLINE SENESI - Siena - Trials event
3.6.1951

Liberio Petrozzi	7th
Elio Bandini	10th

LIÈGES-MILAN-LIÈGES - Long distance event (2,292 km)
10.6.1951

3 Onorato Francone	1st 125 cm^3
Onorato Francone	22nd overall

6th MILANO-TARANTO
24.6.1951

Guerino Mantovani	15th 125 cm^3
Osvaldo Abbate	18th 125 cm^3
Guerino Mantovani	37th overall
Osvaldo Abbate	50th overall

DUE MARI - Sanremo - Trials event
23.6.1951

Ovidio Agosti	1st
Angelo Troisi	1st
Onorato Francone	1st
Guglielmo Strada	1st
Benvenuto Brogini	52nd

Gianni Zonca	52nd
Giovanni Fumagalli	52nd
Guerino Mantovani	52nd

4th CIRCUITO DI SAN FERMO - Hillclimb
15.7.1951

Guerino Mantovani	5th

CIRCUITO DI LISSONE - Speed event
22.7.1951

Gianni Zonca	2nd

TROFEO DI MACERATA - IMF speed event
29.7.1951

Gianni Zonca	8th

TROFEO OROBICO - Bergamo - IMF trials event
29.7.1951

Pietro Carissoni	1st
Gandossi	1st
G. Carlo Rossi	12th
Achille Rumi	17th
Russi	22nd

CAVALCATA DELLE DOLOMITI - Trials event
5.8.1951

Pietro Carissoni	1st
Armando Bombardini	1st
Angelo Troisi	1st
Otello Spadoni	1st
Gianni Zonca	1st
Ottorino Radin	25th
Vittorio Tonello	48th

Olindo Celli	63th
Marcello Corrà	70th
Prize for Industry	1st

1st GIRO DELL'ALTO LARIO - Lecco - Trials event
5.9.1951

Fausto Palombi	1st

CIRCUITO DI LUINO - Speed event
August 1951

Osvaldo Abbate	5th

QUATTRO VALICHI ALPINI - Edolo (Brescia) - Trials event
26.8.1951

Pietro Carissoni	2nd
Angelo Troisi	2nd
Guglielmo Strada	7th
Rino Prati	10th

4th VALLI BERGAMASCHE - Bergamo - National trials event
2.9.1951

Angelo Troisi	2nd
Gianni Zonca	4th
Guglielmo Strada	6th
Onorato Francone	9th
Gianni Fumagalli	23rd
Team	1st

CIRCUITO CAVARZESE - Veneto - Speed event
2.9.1951

Romualdo Zubiani	3rd
Ottorino Radini	4th
Mario Barbieri	5th

Angelo Troisi at the 4th Valichi Alpini event, held on the 26th August 1951, where he came in second equal aboard a Rumi "Sport 125" trials machine.

The identification plate assigned to all the competitors in the 26th Six Days event; naturally, the number in the centre is the race number.

26th INTERNATIONAL SIX DAYS
Varese - IMF International trials event
18-23.9.1951

119	Guglielmo Strada	Gold medal
105	Onorato Francone	Diploma

TRE VALICHI - Sanremo - Trials event
30.9.1951

Augusto Corradi	4th
Eugenio Todisco	6th

TROFEO MANZONI - Voghera - Trials event
7.10.1951

Guglielmo Strada	1st
Angelo Troisi	1st
Benito L'Abruzzi	8th

CRITERIUM DI CHIUSURA ALDRIGHETTI
Milano - Trials event
October 1951

Angelo Troisi	1st
Benito L'Abruzzi	21st
Guglielmo Strada	23rd

1st LIQUIGAS TROPHY - Bergamo - Trials championship event
14.10.1951

Angelo Gandossi	4th
G. Carlo Rossi	5th
Achille Rumi	7th
Gianni Zonca	9th
G. Mario Paleari	11th
Ercole Nani	12th

COPPA ALDO BASSI - Cidneo track - Brescia - Speed event
November 1951

20	Angelo Troisi	1st
	Rino Prati	5th

158

The prestigious Scudo del Sud Trophy was won by Rumi with four riders taking full points in the 1952 edition of this murderously tough trials event. The race was held in the twelve provinces whose coats of arms are represented on the trophy. As well as the Trophy, Rumi also won the President on the Republic's Cup, awarded to the winning marque.

1952

TROFEO ALDRIGHETTI - Milano - Trials event
16.3.1952

Domenico Cavalli	1st
Bruno Romano	1st
Miro Riva	1st
Pietro Carissoni	2nd
Benito L'Abruzzi	3rd
G. Mario Paleari	3rd
Gallara	3rd
Beniamino Riolfi	3rd
Team	1st

7th PRIMI PASSI - Milano - Trials event
March 1952

Bruno Romano	1st
Guglielmo Strada	1st
Gianni Zonca	1st

Achille Rumi	1st
Beniamino Riolfi	1st
Franco Dall'Ara	1st
Miro Riva	1st
Pietro Carissoni	1st
G. Mario Paleari	1st
Onorato Francone	1st
F. Randi	1st
Mario L'Abruzzi	1st
Team	1st

3rd POZZILLO - ACIREALE - Hillclimb
6.4.1952

Carmelo Faro	2nd
Matteo Marletta	5th

4th VALLI FIORENTINE - Trials event
14.4.1952

Benvenuto Brogini	1st

159

The Rumi team at the 4th Scudo del Sud on the 6th May 1952. Among the riders, standing, there is Ing. Luigi Salmaggi and, kneeling on the left, the famous Vittorina Massano, the only woman to win a significant number of events (riding both Rumis and Mondials) in what was exclusively a man's world.

6th TROFEO DEI LAGHI - Trials event
April 1952

Claudio Borella	1st
Domenico Cavalli	1st
Costanzo Daminelli	1st
Beniamino Riolfi	1st
Gianni Zonca	1st
Miro Riva	1st
Pietro Carissoni	1st
Guglielmo Strada	1st
Bruno Romano	1st

COPPA RATICOSA - Trials event
23.4.1952

Franco Dall'Ara	1st
Alberto Gandossi	1st

2nd LIQUIGAS TROPHY - Bergamo - Provincial trials event
1.5.1952

Achille Rumi	1st
Franco Dall'Ara	1st
G. Mario Paleari	1st
Dino Angioletti	1st
Pietro Carissoni	28th

4th SCUDO DEL SUD - Foggia - National trials event
6.5.1952

	Pietro Carissoni	1st
70	Domenico Cavalli 1st	
	Miro Riva	1st
13	Bruno Romano	1st
	Team	1st

TROFEO CITTÀ DI FERRARA - Trials event
11.5.1952

Carlo Ferretti	1st
Alberto Gargiani	1st
Filiberto Brunelli	1st

5th TROFEO CIRCUITO DI VIAREGGIO - Speed event
11.5.1952

Gianni Bianchi	5th

3rd CIRCUITO CITTÀ DI ARCO - Trento - Speed event
18.5.1952

Marino Vertemati	3rd
Odoardo Guerrieri	5th

The Rumi team at the start of the 5th Valli Bergamasche on the 2nd June 1952. From left to right, Tino Gandossi, Gianmario Paleari, Miro Riva, Domenico Fenocchio, Guglielmo Strada, Bruno Romano, Domenico Cavalli and Franco Dall'Ara.

3rd CIRCUITO DEL CIDNEO - Brescia - Hillclimb
May 1952

Angelo Troisi	1st

3rd GIRO DELL'UMBRIA - Trials event
May 1952

Faina	1st
Amici	1st
Santioni	1st
Team	1st

1st CIRCUITO DEL PO - Cremona - Speed event
May 1952

Bruno Romano	4th
Gianni Bianchi	5th

GIRO DEL SESTRIERE - National trials event
25.5.1952

Aristide Armini	1st
Giuseppe Gerosa	1st
Domenico Cavalli	34th

CIRCUITO DI SAN SECONDO - Asti - 2nd Div. speed event
1.6.1952

Gianni Zonca	1st
Gianni Bianchi	3rd
Renzo Genevini	5th
Tomasia	10th

5th VALLI BERGAMASCHE - Bergamo - National trials event
2nd section

2.6.1952

29	Bruno Romano	1st
67	Miro Riva	3rd
41	Pietro Carissoni	7th
72	Guglielmo Strada	13th
37	Domenico Fenocchio	32nd
	Team	2nd

VOLTRI-TURCHINO - Hillclimb
8.6.1952

2	Gianni Zonca	1st
11	Gianni Bianchi	3rd
	Carlo Mori	4th
	Aldo Mantero	6th

Left, Bruno Romano and his "Gobbetto" at the start of the 1952 Milano-Taranto, held on the 14th and 15th June. Romano came third in the 125 class. On the facing page, left, Gianni Zonca wears the victor's laurels after winning the Circuito di San Secondo at Asti on the 1st of June 1952; right, Gianni Bianchi during the Voltri-Turchino event of the 8th August 1952, where he came third.

7th MILANO-TARANTO
14-15.6.1952

154	Bruno Romano	3rd 125 cm³
	Marino Vertemati	8th 125 cm³
150	Ottorino Radini	13th 125 cm³
151	Pietro Carissoni	14th 125 cm³
119	Aristide Armini	20th 125 cm³

CIRCUIT DE LA CHAMBRE - Belgium - Track speed event
June 1952

Rousselle	1st

SASSI-SUPERGA - Hillclimb
19.6.1952

31	Bruno Romano	1st
32	Gianni Zonca	2nd

TROFEO DELL'AUTODROMO
Monza - up to 500 cm³ class speed event
20.6.1952

21	Gianni Zonca	7th 125 Comp.
22	Luigi Sabbatini	10th 125 Comp.
20	Gianni Bianchi	11th 125 Comp.

Right, Gianni Zonca and Bruno Romano at the 1952 Sassi-Superga; far right, Bruno Romano aboard his "Gobbetto" at the prize giving ceremony.

TRIFOGLIO DELLA TOSCANA - National trials event
20.6.1952

	Vittorina Massano	1st
23	Miro Riva	1st
36	Guglielmo Strada	1st
56	Domenico Cavalli	1st
61	Bruno Romano	1st
	Pietro Carissoni	1st
	Chiavazza	43rd
	Team	1st

5th GIRO DELLA CAMPANIA - Team trials event
29.6.1952

Team: Abete-Busti-Caramiello 1st
Team: Roversi-Liberti-Santoro 19th

TROFEO MACERATA - Provincial trials event
29.6.1952

Franco Startoni	1st
Luigi Siatti	1st
Pelo Pardi	1st
Astro Nardi	1st

PONTE ADIGE - Mendola - Hillclimb
6.7.1952

Sergio Bertoletti	4th
Nicola Boventa	5th

3rd COPPA CITTÀ DI PERUGIA
Italian speed championship
6.7.1952

Bruno Romano	1st

Top left, the gold medal awarded to Miro Riva, voted the best rider of 1952; top right, Vittorina Massano and Domenico Cavalli (below), during the Due Giorni event held near Rome in the July of 1952: they came in fifteenth equal.

COPPA DAMIANI - Perugia speed champioship
6.7.1952

| | Ennio Ambrosi | 1st |
| | Prosperi | 2nd |

CIRCUITO DI LANCIANO - Speed event
July 1952

| | Dario Basso | 1st 125 Sport |

TWO DAYS - Rome - IMF Trophy trials event
12.7.1952

	Miro Riva	1st
	Pietro Carissoni	9th
50	Domenico Cavalli	15th
58	Vittorina Massano	15th
	Bruno Romano	22nd
	Guglielmo Strada	27th

Gianni Zonca with mechanic Gianni Spreafico waiting for the off at the Circuito di Pistoia on the 13th July 1952. On the facing page, the Giro della Lucania, 16th August 1952: Domenico Cavalli - who was to finish 1st equal overall - at a check point.

CIRCUITO DI PISTOIA - 2nd Div. speed event
13.7.1952

| 16 Gianni Zonca | 1st |
| Renzo Genevini | 8th |

SORRENTO-SANT'AGATA - Hillclimb
13.7.1952

Vincenzo Rippa	1st
Giuseppe Parisi	2nd
Francesco Russo	9th

TROFEO 3 VALLI - Turin - Italian championship trials event
27.7.1952

Armini	1st
Candanno	1st
Orusa	1st

CIRCUITO DI CAVARZERE - Speed event
July 1952

| Bruno Romano | 1st |
| Gaetano Conti | 2nd |

TROFEO WÜHRER - Brescia - Italian championship trials event
July 1952

Angelo Troisi	1st
Rino Prati	12th
B. Parisio	14th
Pietro Carissoni	18th
Franco Dall'Ara	24th
O. Radin	26th
Team	1st

CIRCUITO DI BORGOLAVEZZARO - Speed event
July 1952

Mario Vertemati	1st

CIRCUITO DI CHIAVARI - 2nd Div. speed event
July 1952

Angelo Bianchi	7th

CIRCUITO DELLA RIVIERA
San Benedetto del Tronto - 2nd Div. hillclimb
27.7.1952

Gianni Zonca	1st
Angelo Troisi	2nd

CIRCUITO DI AVEZZANO - Speed event
July/August 1952

Gaetano Conti	1st

WARSAGE 24 HOURS - Belgium - Speed event
August 1952

20	Oliver-Croes	3rd (up to 175 cm³ class)
	Meert-Delannois	6th (up to 175 cm³ class)

CIRCUIT DE LA CHAMBRE - Belgium - Speed event
August 1952

Freddy Roussel	1st 125 Sport

GIRO DELLA LUCANIA - IMF trials event
16.8.1952

Pietro Carissoni	1st
Domenico Cavalli	1st
Miro Riva	1st
Bruno Romano	1st
Domenico Strada	1st

The fourth edition of the Arco di Adriano Santa Maria Capua Vetere event: Orlando Ciceroni, nicknamed "the Little Roman", gives Zonca's mount a final pre-race once over.

Gianni Zonca	1st
Rino Prati	17th
Team	1st

4th ARCO DI ADRIANO
S. Maria Capua Vetere - 2nd Div. speed event
August 1952

| 28 | Vincenzo Rippa | 4th |

COPPA PESCARA - 2nd Div. speed event
24.8.1952

| Bruno Romano | 2nd |
| Gianni Bianchi | 3rd |

4th VALICHI ALPINI - National trials event
September 1952

Ugo Bertoli	7th
Onorato Francone	9th
B. Parisio	13th
Paroli	14th
Mantelli	22nd

PONTEDECIMO-GIOVI - Hillclimb
7.9.1952

Giuseppe Iguera	2nd M.S.D.
Gianni Zonca	3rd M.S.D.
Ettore Biasetti	5th M.S.D.
Sciacca	9th M.S.D.
Gianni Zonca	2nd Sport
Gianni Bianchi	3rd Sport
Angelo Bianchi	4th Sport

CHARF - Morocco - Track speed event

| Guido Guarnieri | 1st 125 Sport |

CAVALCATA DELLE DOLOMITI - Trials event
7.9.1952

Pietro Carissoni	1st
Fabio Dorigoni	1st
G. Mario Paleari	1st
Nicola Bovolenta	11th
Onorato Francone	11th
Giuseppe Martelli	16th
Ugo Bertoli	24th
Beniamino Riolfi	24th

27th I.S.D.T. - Bad Aussee - Austria - IMF trials event
18-23.9.1952

| 29 | Miro Riva | Silver medal |
| 37 | Pietro Carissoni | Bronze medal |

Domenico Cavalli during the 27th International Six Days Trial event, held from the 18th to the 23rd of September 1952.

169

Another two picture of the 1952 International Six Days Trial. Above, Miro Riva, who won the bronze medal; below, silver medal winner Pietro Carissoni; on the facing page, below, Miro Riva's silver medal.

Left, Angelo Troisi standing beside Rumi "Gobbetto" 125, with which he won the Circuito del Cidneo for the second time.

TROFEO BLANDI - Naples - Speed event
September 1952

Vincenzo Rippa	1st
Vincenzo Topo	2nd
Federico Perfetto	6th
Antonio Caramiello	9th

CIRCUITO DEL CIDNEO - Brescia - Coppa A. Bassi
November 1952

18 Angelo Troisi	1st Comp.

At the end of the 1952 season:

Bruno Romano	won the Italian trials championship aboard a Rumi 125.
Miro Riva	was runner-up in the Italian trials championship aboard a Rumi 125.
Moto Rumi	won the Italian trials championship manufacturers' title.

171

Bruno Romano portrayed with the new "Gran Turismo" 200 cm^3 on the occasion of the 8th Primi Passi event, held on the 15th of March 1953.

1953

TROFEO ALDRIGHETTI - Milano - National trials event
6.3.1953

Ovidio Agosto	1st
Romagnoni	17th
Ugo Bertoli	17th
Vasco Loro	17th
Nino Pesenti	49th
Team	3rd

8th PRIMI PASSI - Milano - Trials event
15.3.1953

G. Mario Paleari	1st
Pietro Carissoni	1st
Miro Riva	1st
Bruno Romagnoni	1st
Ugo Bertoli	1st
Ovidio Agosti	1st
Lino Scarpellini	1st
Claudio Borella	1st
Franco Dall'Ara	1st

Guglielmo Strada	1st
Onorato Francone	1st
Nino Pesenti	1st
Primo Basilico	1st
Angelo Troisi	1st
118 Bruno Romano	1st 200 cm^3
Team	1st

TRE VALLI VARESINE - Varese - Trials event
March 1953

Onorato Francone	1st
Gianni Fumagalli	1st
Ugo Bertoli	1st
Orlando Gerini	1st
Dino Raffo	1st
Natale Garavaglia	1st
Team	1st

CIRCUITO DI S. GIUSEPPE - Parma - Speed event
March 1953

| Mario Galliani | 1st |
| Giuseppe Bertozzi | 2nd |

1st GIRO MOTOCICLISTICO D'ITALIA
30.3-3.4.1953

156	Michele Ronchei	3rd 125 cm^3
156	Michele Ronchei	4th overall
	The Necchi Crash Helmet Co. Team 1st	
201	Miro Riva	
158	Bruno Romano	
170	Onorato Francone	

The 5th of April 1953, the 1st Giro Motociclistico d'Italia: Bruno Romano (no. 158) and Gianni Zonca (no. 259) wait to have the seals attached to their bikes in the parc fermé at Bologna.

2nd COPPA DELLA RATICOSA -Trials event
April 1953

	Pietro Carissoni	1st 175 cm^3
	Miro Riva	1st 175 cm^3
81	Guglielmo Strada	1st 175 cm^3
	Angelo Troisi	1st
	Gianni Zonca	1st
	Team	1st

5th VALLI FIORENTINE - Provincial trials championship
12.4.1953

| Luciano Piccini | 12th |
| Mauro Cintolesi | 19th |

WATERLOO - Belgium
April 1953

| Sosman | 1st 125 Comp. |
| Belgian championship 125 class | |

Gianmario Paleari (no. 9), at the San Giacomo bend during the Circuito delle Mura event, held in Bergamo on the 10th of May 1953: Paleari came sixth in the second class of this national speed event, while Gianni Zonca, behind Paleari in the photo, retired with mechanical problems.

TROFEO GIANFERRARI - Reggio Emilia - IMF trials event
April 1953

22	G. Franco Saini	1st
27	Ovidio Agosti	1st
	Dietrich Serafini	1st
	Michele Ronchei	1st
	Angelo Troisi	1st
	Guglielmo Strada	1st
	Pietro Carissoni	1st
	Team	1st

11th TROFEO CITTÀ DI BERGAMO - National trials event
25.4.1953

Angelo Troisi	2nd
G. Franco Saini	7th
Gianni Zonca	8th
Miro Riva	9th
Lino Scarpellini	14th
Dino Angioletti	18th
Rino Selvaggi	21st
Team	2nd

TROFEO A. SOLZI - Soresina - Div. 3 Sport class speed event
April 1953

Mario Galliani	1st
Ernesto Brambilla	4th
Giuseppe Bertozzi	7th

GIRO CASTELLI ROMANI - Provincial trials championship
3.5.1953

Sergio Mattia	1st
Roberto Vigorito	1st
V. Messier	1st
Armando Anella	1st

The 1953 Circuito delle Mura: top, winner Franco Dall'Ara tackles the San Lorenzo bend; above, Gian Franco Saini, who came eighth.

G. Lello	1st
C. Giuliani	1st
A. Mattia	1st

2nd MARANELLO-SERRAMAZZONI - 2nd Div. hillclimb
May 1953

| Ezio Paltrinieri | 1st |

COPPA PROVINCIA DI MILANO - 3rd Div. speed event
3.5.1953

| Ovidio Agosti | 2nd |

CIRCUITO DELLE MURA
Bergamo - Provincial championship speed event
10.5.1953

4	Franco Dall'Ara	1st
	Pietro Carissoni	2nd
22	Pietro Brignoli	4th
8	G. Franco Saini	8th
	Sergio Villa	9th

2nd Div. National speed championship

| 9 | G. Mario Paleari | 6th |

CIRCUITO DI PESCARA - 3rd Div. speed event
May 1953

| Tullio Tavarozzi | 2nd |

TROFEO ITALO PALLI
Casale Monferrato - IMF trials event - 2nd section
14.5.1953

Bruno Romano	1st
Miro Riva	1st 175 cm^3
Angelo Troisi	1st 175 cm^3
Pietro Carissoni	18th 175 cm^3
Onorato Francone	28th 200 cm^3
Dietrich Serafini	31st
G. Franco Serafini	36th
Ovidio Agosti	39th
Team	3rd

CIRCUITO DI FROSINONE - 2nd Div. National speed event
14.5.1953

| 58 | Gianni Zonca | 2nd |

| 60 | Vincenzo Rippa | 3rd |

GRASSTRACK SPEED MEETING - Belp - Switzerland
May 1953

Mario Della Santa   1st 125 cm³

7th TROFEO DEI LAGHI - Trials event
17.5.1953

Dario Basso	1st
Ovidio Agosti	1st
Bruno Romano	1st
Onorato Francone	1st
Miro Riva	1st
Lino Scarpellini	10th
I. Aldrighetti	23rd

CIRCUITO DI CAMERINO - 3rd Div. Provincial speed event
18.5.1953

Enzo Antognini   1st

2nd Div. National speed championship

| 9 | Gianni Zonca | 1st |
| | G. Mario Paleari | 4th |

TROFEO BERTOLI - Brescia - 3rd section IMF trials event
23-24.5.1953

Angelo Troisi   4th 200 cm³

DORIA-CRETO - Genoa - 2nd Div. hillclimb
25.5.1953

Luciano Testa   1st 125 Sport

Above, the starting grid at the 1953 Circuito delle Mura: from the left, Gianni Zonca, mechanic Dino Ballerini, and Gianmario Paleari. Left, Enzo Rippa during the Circuito di Frosinone of the 14th of May 1953, when he took third place.

The 14th May 1953, the Circuito di Frosinone: rider no. 60 is Enzo Rippa an no. 58 is Gianni Zonca; on the extreme right a privateer bearing no. 72 gives Rippa's works "Gobbetto" a perplexed look.

Ettore Biasetti	2nd 125 Sport
Mario Leonardini	4th
Angelo Bianchi	1st 125 Comp.

CIRCUITO DI JESI - 2nd and 3rd Div. speed event

Vincenzo Antognini	3rd
Angelo Brazzini	4th
Candido Riderelli	6th
Franco Martelli	8th

COPPA DEL MARE - Genoa - International speed event
June 1953

| Angelo Bianchi | 5th |

PREMIO NAZIONALE SANREMO
Ospitaletti Autodrome - 3rd Div. speed event
14.6.1953

| Roberto Damiani | 4th 125 cm^3 |
| Aquilini Franchini | 6th |

VOLTRI-TURCHINO - Hillclimb
June 1953

| Angelo Bianchi | 1st 125 Comp. |
| Ettore Biasetti | 1st 125 Comp. |

CIRCUITO DI MONTEBELLUNA - Veneto - Speed event
June 1953

| Vito Clerici | 1st |

178

The large photo shows the Rumi squad at the 1953 Circuito di Frosinone: Gianni Zonca is between the mechanics Dino Ballerini (on the left) and Orlando Ciceroni (on the right). Below, Gianni Zonca rides a "Gobbetto" equipped with an external magneto at the Circuito del Camerino of the 18th of May 1953.

CIRCUITO DI TRECATE - Speed event
June 1953

    Ernesto Brambilla   1st

CIRCUITO DI COLLEMAGGIO - Speed event
June 1953

    Giulio Rotellini   1st

RECCO-USCIO - Hillclimb
June 1953

    Angelo Bianchi   1st

Right, the souvenir medal that was awarded to all those who took part in the exhausting Schaerbeek 24 Hours event in Belgium. In the centre of the page, Gianni Zonca in action at the Circuito dei Viali on the 28th of June 1953.

SCHAERBEEK 24 HOURS - Belgium - Trials event
20.6.1953

Angelo Troisi	1st	175 cm³
		Gold medal
Angelo Troisi	3rd	overall

CIRCUITO DI CORTONA - 2nd Div. speed event
June 1953

Mauro Cintolesi	1st

WARSAGE 24 HOURS - Belgium - Speed event
June 1953

Romano-Troisi	1st	125 cm³
Romano-Troisi	7th	overall

8th MILANO-TARANTO
22.6.1953

Dario Basso	8th 125 Sport
O. Ghiro	14th 125 Sport
Pietro Carissoni	17th 125 Sport
E. Ambrosi	20th 125 Sport
G. Cattini	21st 125 Sport
Ennio Ferrari	22nd 125 Sport
Angelo Troisi	23rd 125 Sport
Onorato Francone	35th 125 Sport
Elio Ferrari	44th 125 Sport
F. La Torre	45th 125 Sport

CIRCUITO DI LERICI - Hillclimb
June 1953

Renato Sartori	1st

3rd CIRCUITO DEI VIALI - Pinerolo - 2nd Div. speed event
28.6.1953

Gianni Zonca	1st
G. Mario Paleari	4th

8th GIRO DEL QUADRIFOGLIO
Castellazzo Bormida - Trials event
29.6.1953

Carlo Poggi	1st
Team Bianchi-Biasetti-Testa	1st

VIGOLO VATTARO - Trento - Trials event
5.7.1953

Fabio Dorigoni	2nd 125 Group C
F. Bovalenta	3rd
Umberto Conci	4th
Remo Giorgetti	7th
Danilo Ferrari	8th
Carmelo Stedile	13th
Adolfo Giogetti	15th

HEDEMORA - Sweden - Track speed event - Senior Div.
11-12.7.1953

Moto Rumi	2nd 125 Comp.
Moto Rumi	3rd 125 Comp.
Moto Rumi	4th 125 Comp.

Junior speed event

Moto Rumi	1st 125 Sport
Moto Rumi	2nd 125 Sport
Moto Rumi	3rd 125 Sport

2nd COPPA TOSCO-UMBRA - Trials event
12.7.1953

Sergio Conti	1st
Mauro Cintolesi	1st
Benvenuto Brogini	1st
Angiolo Artioli	1st
Luciano Piccini	1st

The start of the Circuito dei Viali: Paleari and Zonca, respectively numbers 6 and 7, assisted by mechanics Romanino and Angelo Colleoni.

181

Two shots from the Lièges-Milan-Lièges event held between the 19th and the 23rd of July 1953. Near right, gold medal winner Angelo Troisi. Far right, Troisi and Bruno Romano pose alongside the Rumi 125 with the special swinging arm frame identical to the one fitted to the second series "Gobbetto".

23rd LIÈGES-MILAN-LIÈGES
19-23.7.1953

90	Bruno Romano	1st	125 cm³
			Gold medal
83	Angelo Troisi	19th	200 cm³
			Gold medal
59	Bruno Carissoni	26th	200 cm³
			Silver medal

VOSTKUSTL - SWEDEN - Track speed event
19.7.1953

| Moto Rumi | 3rd 125 cm³ |
| Moto Rumi | 4th 125 cm³ |

5th COPPA CITTÀ DI PISTOIA - 3rd Div. speed event
26.7.1953

| Mauro Cintolesi | 2nd |
| Romano Giannoni | 6th |

1st CIRCUITO DEL VERGANTE - National trials event
2.8.1953

| Claudio Barcella | 1st |
| Andrea Zonca | 12th |

5th COPPA DELLE BALEARI - Marina di M.
2nd Div. speed event
2.8.1953

The 1953 Lièges-Milan-Lièges. Above, Luigi Salmaggi and silver medal winner Pietro Carissoni, during the awards ceremony. Below, the Rumi team: from left to right, we can recognize Angelo Troisi, Pietro Carissoni, Miro Riva, and Bruno Romano.

From the left, Pietro Carissoni, Bruno Romano, and Angelo Troisi aboard the new Rumi "Gran Turismo" 200cm^3 at the Valli Bergamasche event on the 9th August 1953. Carissoni took twelfth place, while the other two were seventh equal.

| G. Mario Paleari | 2nd |
| Gianni Zonca | 7th |

BLEKINGEL - Sweden - Track speed event - Senior Div.
2.8.1953

| Moto Rumi | 3rd 125 Comp. |
| Moto Rumi | 4th 125 Comp. |

Junior Div.

| Moto Rumi | 3rd 125 Sport |

6th VALLI BERGAMASCHE
Bergamo - National trials event
9.8.1953

| 23 | Miro Riva | 1st 125 cm^3 |

81	Angelo Troisi	7th 200 cm^3
85	Bruno Romano	7th 200 cm^3
83	Pietro Carissoni	12th 200 cm^3
79	Guglielmo Strada	20th 200 cm^3
	Team	2st

COPPA DELLA CONSUMA - Hillclimb
9.8.1953

Mauro Cintolesi	2nd
Piero Frescobaldi	3rd
Piero Coppini	4th
Ciriano Innocenti	5th
Sergio Conti	7th
Benvenuto Brogini	10th

CIRCUITO DI PESCARA - 2nd Div. speed event
August 1953

Giovanni Ridenti	4th
Tullio Tavarozzi	5th
Morgia	8th
De Matteis	11th

CIRCUITO DI CAVARZERE - 2nd Div. speed event
August 1953

Angelo Troisi	1st

8th CIRCUITO CITTÀ DI SPOLETO - 2nd Div. speed event
August 1953

Gianni Zonca	4th
Aldo Brazzini	5th

CIRCUITO DI LUINO - 2nd Div. speed event
16.8.1953

G. Mario Paleari	2nd
Gianni Zonca	3rd

CERNOBBIO-BISBINO - Hillclimb
21.8.1953

Ernesto Brambilla	1st
Gianni Bianchi	3rd
Aquilino Franchini	4th
Giovanni Cattini	10th

ALMERIA - Spain - Speed event
August 1953

Renato Montalbano	1st

MOTOCROSS DI BIENNE - Switzerland
August 1953

Mario Della Santa	1st

9th QUATTRO VALICHI ALPINI - Edolo - Trials event
23.8.1953

Dario Basso	1st
Bruno Romano	1st 200 cm³
Guglielmo Strada	1st 200 cm³
Aldo Zecca	1st
Miro Riva	15th
Elio Pedretti	18th
Angelo Troisi	18 200 cm³
Pietro Carissoni	25th 200 cm³
Team	3rd

Lino Scarpellini at the start of the 1953 Valli Bergamasche astride a first series Rumi "Regolarità" 125.

185

CITTÀ DI LECCO – Nighttime trials event
30.8.1953

Angelo Troisi	1st

CIRCUITO DI MACERATA - Speed event
30.8.1953

Tullio Tabarozzi	1st
Giulio Rotellini	2nd
Giovanni Florian	6th
Aldo Brazzini	9th
Antonio Zaffiri	11th
Dario Marcucci	12th

CIRCUITO DELL'ACQUATRAVERSA
Rome - Speed event
30.8.1953

Roberto Vigorito	5th
Sergio Mattia	6th
Enea Cristofori	8th
Ennio Gherardi	10th

CIRCUITO DI ASOLA - Speed event
August 1953

Odoardo Guerrieri Gonzaga	1st

CIRCUITO DI CASTELLAMARE - 2nd Div. speed event
September 1953

Edoardo Rippa	2nd
Francesco Russo	3rd

KRISTIANSTAD CIRCUIT - Sweden
Senior speed event
13.9.1953

Moto Rumi	3rd
Moto Rumi	4th

Junior speed event

Moto Rumi	2nd
Moto Rumi	3rd

TRENTO-MONTE BONDONE - Hillclimb
20.9.1953

Umberto Conci	7th
Gino Zanola	8th

CIRCUITO DI CIVITAVECCHIA - Speed event
20.9.1953

Roberto Vigorito	2nd
Armando Anella	3rd
Giovanni Morgia	4th
Amicucci	6th

PONTEDECIMO-GIOVI - Hillclimb
September 1953

Angelo Bianchi	1st

26th SASSI-SUPERGA - Hillclimb
27.9.1953

19	Bruno Romano	1st
	Barbero	9th

CIRCUITO DELLA FORTEZZA - Florence - 3rd Div.
27.9.1953

Mauro Cintolesi	3rd
Piero Coppini	4th
Piero Frescobaldi	5th
Luciano Piccini	7th

CIRCUITO DEL CASTELLO
Castelfranco Veneto - 2nd Div. speed event
27.9.1953

15	Gianni Zonca	1st
	Cesare Ferrari	6th

GAVERINA - Bergamo trials championship
27.9.1953

	Lino Scarpellini	1st
31	Miro Riva	1st
	Pietro Carissoni	1st 200 cm³
	Dario Basso	1st 200 cm³

CIRCUITO CITTÀ DI VERONA - 2nd Div. speed event
October 1953

Ettore Corti	1st
Ernesto Brambilla	4th
Edoardo Gonzaga	5th
Sardo Gerosa	6th

CRITERIUM D'AUTUNNO - Desio - Trials event
4.10.1953

Miro Riva	1st
Bruno Romano	6th
Dario Basso	7th
Team	1st

ANFA - Casablanca - North Africa - Speed event
11.10.1953

83	Massimiliano Milanese	1st

CRITERIUM DI CHIUSURA - Milano - Trials event
11.10.1953

103	Bruno Romano	1st
	Angelo Troisi	1st
	Guglielmo Strada	15th 200 cm³
	Guido Fornoni	15th
	Renato Romagnoni	21st
	Nino Pesenti	35th
	Isidoro Maccarone	52nd

CIRCUITO DEL CIDNEO - Brescia - Speed event
1.11.1953

Angelo Troisi	1st
Bresciani	2nd

CIRCUITO DI LATINA - Speed event
November 1953

Roberto Vigorito	1st

TROFEO MUCCIARELLI
Rome - Regional trials championship
December 1953

Armando Anella	1st
Amerigo Gobbi	1st
Roberto Vigorito	1st
Fausto Palamini	1st
Sergio Mattia	1st
Roberto Mattia	7th

At the end of the 1953 season:

Miro Riva	riding a Rumi, won the 125 cm³ class of the Bergamo trials championship.
Sosman	riding a Rumi, won the 125 cm³ class of the Belgian speed championship.

The Trofeo Aldrighetti of the 7th March 1954. The Rumi team on the 200 cm³ class: form the left, Guglielmo Strada, Bruno Romano, and Onorato Francone. Romano's bike (no. 84) was a special Rumi 200 with teledraulic forks.

1954

4th TROFEO ALDRIGHETTI - National trials event
7.3.1954

32	Dario Basso	1st
34	Pietro Carissoni	1st
33	Mario Riva	1st

Penalized:

83	Onorato Francone	200 cm³
	Enrico Gerosa	
	Antonio Sala	

Guido Fornoni
Lino Scotti

TROFEO FIORENTINO - Florence - Provincial trials event
3.7.1954

	Dino Salvatoni	1st 125 cm³
41	Piero Frescobaldi	1st 125 cm³
42	Giorgio Bagnoli	1st 125 cm³
43	Cabruccio Cabrucci	1st 125 cm³
	Mauro Sestini	12th 125 cm³
	Mauro Cintolesi	1st 200 cm³
	Team	1st

9th PRIMI PASSI - Provincial trials event
14.3.1954

	Miro Riva	1st
	Bruno Romano	1st
	Guglielmo Strada	1st
	Vittorio Gerosa	1st
43	Angelo Troisi	1st Silver medal
	Onorato Francone	1st
40	Pietro Carissoni	61st
	Dario Basso	68th 200 cm³
	Team	2nd

COPPA U.C.I.M.I. - Imola - 3rd Div. speed event
21.3.1954

Pietro Carissoni	4th
Floridan	6th
Conti	7th

CIRCUITO DI SIENA - Speed event
March 1954

Piero Frescobaldi	1st

The full Rumi team photographed in March 1954. Donnino Rumi is third from the right in the second row.

189

Two pictures of the Giro Motociclistico d'Italia, held on the 3rd of April 1954. Right, Gianni Zonca at the Bergamo check point. Below, Bruno Romano leaps into the saddle of his refuelled "Bicarburatore" before riding on to a 4th place in the 125 class.

2nd GIRO MOTOCICLISTICO D'ITALIA
3.4.1954

311	Luigi Ciai	2nd 125 cm^3
399	Roberto Vigorito	3rd 125 cm^3
305	Bruno Romano	3th 125 cm^3
313	Dario Basso	6th 125 cm^3
319	Miro Riva	7th 125 cm^3
	Giulio Rotellini	8th 125 cm^3
	Guglielmo Strada	10th 125 cm^3
	Buongiorno	12th 125 cm^3
	Pezzi	14th 125 cm^3
	Pietro Carissoni	16th 125 cm^3
285	Gianni Zonca	23rd 125 cm^3
	Danilo Ferrari	26th 125 cm^3
	Caramiello	27th 125 cm^3
	Onorato Francone	30th 125 cm^3
	Porta	40th 125 cm^3
	Team	2nd

190

Above, Gianni Zonca at the 1954 Motogiro. Below, Zonca again, this time in the 1954 Milano-Taranto event, where he came fifth in the 125 Competition class.

Above, three Rumi's best riders in action during the 1954 Motogiro. Right, the Motogiro again; Miro Riva stands by his "Bicarburatore" 125 as the lead seals are applied in the parc fermé in Bologna.

Left, Miro Riva at a check point during the Moto-giro. Right, it's the 20th of June 1954 and the ninth Milano-Taranto event: an exhausted Gianni Zonca arrives at the finish.

Two pictures from the 1954 Valli Bergamasche. Right, winner Bruno Romano during the night-time stage. Far right, Guglielmo Strada at a check point in front of the historic Cantoniera Veneta at Ca' San Marco.

6th VALLI FIORENTINE - Trials event
25.4.1954

Raffaello Rosati	1st
Mauro Cintolesi	1st
Dino Salvadori	6th
Marino Somigli	13th
Giorgio Magnoli	16th

4th CIRCUITO DELLA FORTEZZA - Siena
3rd Div. speed event
25.4.1954

Piero Frescobaldi	1st
Mauro Cintolesi	6th
Dino Salvadori	8th

CIRCUITO DI FLERO - 3rd Div. speed event
May 1954

Silvano Rinaldi	1st
Pietro Carissoni	2nd
Chierici	6th
Franco Moriggia	7th
Zanola	8th

3rd MARANELLO-SERRAMAZZONI - 3rd Div. hillclimb
1.5.1954

Mauro Cintolesi	4th

CASTELLI ROMANI - Provincial championship trials event
9.5.1954

Baldini	1st
Sergio Mattia	1st
Merolle	1st
Luigi Ciai	1st
Roberto Vigorito	1st
Team	1st

SAN GIULIANO 12 HOURS
Pisa - IMF Italian championship trials event
16.5.1954

	Miro Riva	1st
35	Guglielmo Strada	1st
20	Dario Basso	1st
	Roberto Vigorito	1st
	Bruno Romano	1st
	Pietro Carissoni	1st
	Attilio Pera	1st
	Gianni Zonca	1st
	Team	1st

Another shot of the 1954 Valli Bergamasche: Guglielmo Strada at a check point with Achille Rumi standing alongside.

CIRCUITO DI SAN SECONDO - Asti - 3rd Div. speed event
16.5.1954

 Enzo Mereghetti 1st

CIRCUITO DI JESI - Speed event
16.5.1954

19 Silvano Rinaldi 1st
  Giulio Rotellini 2nd

6th SCUDO DEL SUD - IMF Italian championship trials event
28-30.5.1954

  Miro Riva 1st
32 Bruno Romano 1st
  Guglielmo Strada 1st
  Pietro Carissoni 1st
  Dario Basso 1st
  Roberto Vigorito 1st

Penalized:
 Gianni Zonca

DORIA-CRETO - Genoa - Hillclimb
June 1954

  Luciano Testa 1st 125 Sport
  Agostino Carosio 4th 125 Sport
  Angelo Musso 5th 125 Sport
  Giovanni Albalustra 6th 125 Sport
  Giuseppe Boero 7th 125 Sport
  Giulio Repetto 8th 125 Sport

  Angelo Bianchi 1st 125 Comp.

2nd TROFEO OMOBONO TENNI
Montebelluna - Speed event
June 1954

Secondo Stocco 1st 125 Sport
Luigi Zanola 3rd
Giuseppe Filco 5th
Giovanni Ferracini 6th

1st CIRCUITO DI POSILLIPO - 3rd Div. speed event
June 1954

 Antonio Graziano 2nd
 Giuseppe Parisi 6th

TROFEO OROBICO - Bergamo - National trials event
6.6.1954

16 Gianni Zonca 1st
  Miro Riva 4th
  Dario Basso 6th
  Team 2nd

CIRCUITO DI TREVISO - 3rd Div. speed event
June 1954

 Enzo Mereghetti 1st
 Silvano Ferracini 2nd
 Giuseppe Filira 7th

7th GIRO DELLA CAMPANIA
3rd Div. provincial trials event
June 1954

 Pasquale Abete 1st
 Caramiello 2nd
 Busti 4th

9th MILANO-TARANTO
20.6.1954

 Pietro Carissoni 2nd 125 cm³
 Giulio Rotellini 5th 125 cm³

196

E. Gerosa	10th 125 cm^3
Pezzi	12th 125 cm^3
S. Gerosa	15th 125 cm^3
Davico	24th 125 cm^3
Nebuloni	25th 125 cm^3
Gasperini	27th 125cm^3
Torreggiani	28th 125cm^3

364	Bruno Romano	1st 125 Comp.
	Roberto Vigorito	4th 125 Comp.
349	Gianni Zonca	5th 125 Comp.
	Michele Ronchei	7th 125 Comp.
	Fornoni	8th 125 Comp.
	Miro Riva	9th 125 Comp.
	Onorato Francone	12th 125 Comp.

GIORNATA MOTOCICLISTICA DEL PO
Cremona - 3rd Div. speed event
13.6.1954

Enzo Mereghetti	2nd
Franco Ubbiali	6th

TROFEO NAZIONALE REGOLARITÀ
Gardone - Val Trompia
13.6.1954

E. Bologna	1st

PIAZZOLA SUL BRENTA - 3rd Div. hillclimb
June 1954

Franco Moriggia	1st
Giuseppe Filire	2nd

METTET - Belgium - Speed event
June 1954

Lechardier	1st 125 cm^3

7th VALLI BERGAMASCHE - Bergamo -
2nd section - IMF Italian championship
28.6.1954

29	Bruno Romano	1st
22	Pietro Carissoni	8th
36	Guglielmo Strada	17th
	Team	3rd

COPPA CITTÀ DI JESI - Speed event
27.6.1954

Attilio di Fino	5th

CIRCUITO DI PIAZZOLA - Speed event
June 1954

Franco Moriggia	1st

CIRCUITO DI COLLEMAGGIO - Aquila
2nd Div. speed event
27.6.1954

Bruno Romano	9th
Roberto Vigorito	10th

CIRCUITO DI SAN PIERO AGLIANA
3rd Div. speed event
27.6.1954

Mauro Cintolesi	2nd

4th CIRCUITO DI S. PIERO IN SIEVE
3rd Div. speed event
29.6.1954

Mauro Cintolesi	1st

29th June 1954, Mauro Cintolesi tackles the Circuito di San Piero a Sieve, where he won aboard a Rumi "Bicarburatore".

GIRO DEI MONTI PRENESTINI - Provincial trials event
June 1954

Luigi Ciai	1st
Roberto Vigorito	1st
Sergio Mattia	1st
Team	1st

SASSI-SUPERGA - Hillclimb
July 1954

F. Guerra	4th

TROFEO CITTÀ DI SONDRIO - National trials event
4.7.1954

Aldo Zecca	1st
Stelio Pedretti	1st
A. Finiguerra	1st
Team	1st

RECCO-USCIO - Hillclimb
4.7.1954

Luciano Testa	1st 125 Sport

CORSA DEL MARE - Rome - Speed event
18.7.1954

Roberto Vigorito	2nd 125 Comp.
A. Pampili	3rd 125 Sport

Two pictures (dated 4th of July 1954) from the Circuito di Bäderpreiss in Austria. Above, Raimond Voll. Left, Gianni Zonca, who came fifth on his second series "Gobbetto".

GIRO DELLA SILA - IMF national trials event
18.7.1954

	Giuseppe Taboscio	1st
13	Leonardo Buongiorno	1st
	Pasquale Abete	1st
	Gerolamo Guercia	8th

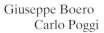

Giuseppe Boero   5th 125 Sport
Carlo Poggi   1st 125 Comp.

TROFEO DELL'ORTO - Seregno - Provincial trials event
11.7.1954

Renato Romagnoni	1st
Angelo Spinelli	2nd
Alberto Sacco	6th
Enrico Gerosa	7th

SWEDISH GRAND PRIX - Hedemora - Track speed event
18.7.1954

2	Giovanni Zonca	2nd 125 Comp.

Above, Mauro Cintolesi at the Circuito di Morisummano, which he won on the 1st of August 1954. Right, a "Bicarburatore" fitted with megaphones during the Loiblpassrennen, a hillclimb event held in Austria. The year was 1954.

16	Rune Hogglund	5th 125 SS.TT
14	Berndt Nilsson	7th 125 SS.TT
9	Eije Wilden	8th 125 SS.TT
	Jan Johnson	11 125 Comp.

7th CERNOBBIO-BISBINO - Hillclimb
25.7.1954

Pietro Carissoni	2nd
Franco Moriggia	6th
Ambrogio Tresoldi	10th

BADEN GRAND PRIX - Austria - Speed event
25.7.1954

| 74 | Giovanni Zonca | 5th 125 Comp. |

3rd COPPA TOSCO-UMBRA - Trials event
25.7.1954

| Mauro Cintolesi | 1st |
| Pietro Frescobaldi | 1st |

SKARPNACKSLOPET - Stockholm - Sweden
July 1954

| 7 | Billy Nicklasson | 1st 125 SS.TT |

CIRCUITO DI CAVARZERE - 2nd Div. speed event
1.8.1954

| Gianni Zonca | 6th |

3rd CIRCUITO DI MORISUMMANO - 2nd Div. speed event
1.8.1954

| Mauro Cintolesi | 1st |
| Pietro Frescobaldi | 2nd |

The 18th July 1954, the Swedish Grand Prix at the Hedemora circuit. Above, Jan Johnsson alongside the 2nd series "Gobbetto" with which he took 11th place; on the right, Berndt Nillson's "Bicarburatore", which took him to 7th place. Below, Gianni Zonca (no. 2) chats with Massimo Ginevrini, on the Mondial, before the start. Zonca's mount is an experimental 2nd series "Gobbetto" with swinging arm rear suspension.

TROFEO WÜHRER - Brescia - Trials event
August 1954

Bruno Romano	4th
Dario Basso	11th
Pietro Carissoni	14th
Team	3rd

RUNDSTRECKENRENNEN
Locarno - Switzerland - Speed event
August 1954

Mario Dalla Santa	1st

7th AGOSTO MONTICIANO - Rome - Hillclimb
15.8.1954

Roberto Vigorito	1st
Armando Anella	2nd
Alvaro Mucci	4th

Zonca makes the final touches to his bike before the start of the Swedish Grand Prix.

Sergio Mattia	5th
Amerigo Gobbi	7th
Luigi Cristofari	9th

28th CIRCUITO DI VERONA - 3rd Div. speed event
22.8.1954

Silvano Rinaldi	1st
Mauro Cintolesi	2nd
Pietro Frescobaldi	3rd
Bruno Gerosa	7th
Sandro Gerosa	10th

CIRCUITO DELLE MURA DI TREVISO
3rd Div. speed event

29.8.1954

Nico Filira	2nd
Secondo Stocco	3rd
Germano Ferracini	4th

3rd CIRCUITO DI SANGEMINI - 2nd Div. speed event
29.8.1954

Roberto Vigorito	5th

CIRCUITO DELLA LANA - Valdagno - Speed event
5.9.1954

Mauro Cintolesi	1st
Pietro Frescobaldi	2nd
Enzo Mereghetti	3rd

CIRCUITO DI VALDAGNO - 2nd Div. speed event
September 1954

Mauro Cintolesi	1st

2nd CIRCUITO DI FLERO - Speed event
September 1954

Enzo Mereghetti	1st

GRASSTRACK SPEED MEETING - Bergamo
9.9.1954

Dario Basso	1st

THE IMOLA 12 HOURS - Team speed event
19.9.1954

Cintolesi-Baglioni	2nd

Winner Mario della Santa on a Rumi "Bicarburatore" with an external magneto at the Rundstreckenrennen (Locarno) speed event in the August 1954.

Pezzi-Rosati	6th

PONTEDECIMO-GIOVI - 2nd Div. hillclimb
19.9.1954

Angelo Bianchi	2nd 125 Comp.
Luciano Testa	2nd 125 Sport

29th INTERNATIONAL SIX DAYS
Llandrindod Wells G.B. - IMF trials event
20-26.9.1954

15	Dario Basso	Gold medal
78	Pietro Carissoni	Gold medal
71	Miro Riva	Gold medal

76	Bruno Romano	Gold medal
	Team	Gold medal

CIRCUITO DI AVEZZANO - Speed event
September 1954

Tullio Tavarozzi	1st

CIRCUITO DI VIMERCATE - Speed event
September 1954

Gian Pietro Zubani	3rd
S. Rinaldi	4th

A few shots from the Rumi album: these photos where taken at the International Six Days Trial event held at Llandrindod Wells (Wales) from the 20th to the 26th of September 1954. Above, the gold medal awarded to Miro Riva by the IMF. Below, Pietro Carissoni, who won a gold medal along with Riva, Basso, and Romano.

In the large central photo, Dario Basso. Above, Bruno Romano. Below, Bruno Romano and Pietro Carissoni take a well-earned breather.

Above, Miro Riva during the International Six Days. Right, the gold medal awarded by the Italian Motorcycle Racers' Association to Miro Riva for his win in the English event.

SEI GIORNI INTERNAZ.
EX-AEQUO
UCMI
1954

7th CIRCUITO DEL TIRRENO - Civitavecchia - Speed event
26.9.1954

Roberto Vigorito	2nd
Belardino Lata	4th
Sergio Merollo	5th

COPPA U.C.M.I. - Monza Autodrome - 3rd Div. speed event
3.10.1954

Gianpiero Zubani	6th 125 cm^3

3rd PROVA CAMPIONATO ROMANO - Trials event

Amerigo Gobbi	1st
Luigi Ciai	1st
Armando Anella	1st
Sergio Mattia	1st

SALITA DELLA CONSUMA - Hillclimb
3.10.1954

Mauro Cintolesi	2nd
Nardi	3rd

TRENTO-MONTE BONDONE - Hillclimb
October 1954

Lodovico Unterholzer	1st

MOTOGIRO TOSCANO - Trials event
10.10.1954

	Pietro Frescobaldi	1st
69	Bruno Romano	4th
	Gianni Zonca	6th

Miro Riva	7th
Mauro Cintolesi	8th
Pietro Carissoni	9th
Dario Basso	11th
Enzo Torregiani	13th
Luigi Davico	15th
Attilio Pera	17th
Luciano Vianello	19th
Silvano Pittini	20th
Team	1st

ARICCIA-ROCCA DI PAPA - Hillclimb
10.10.1954

Roberto Vigorito	1st
Amerigo Gobbi	6th
Fernando Pierotti	7th
Sergio Merollo	8th
"Eros"	10th
Belardino Lata	15th
"La Face"	16th

9th CIRCUITO DI FROSINONE - 3rd Div. speed event
7.11.1954

Giovanni Morgia	2nd
Mario Biondi	4th

At the end of the 1954 season:

Bruno Romano	riding a Rumi 125, was runner-up in the 2nd Div. Italian speed championship.
Roberto Vigorito	riding a Rumi 125, took 9th place in the 2nd Div. Italian speed championship.
Ferruccio Delle Fusine	riding a Rumi, won the Venezuelan national 125 championship.

Above, the Italian Vase team photographed during the Six Days; from the left, the steward Carletto Merlo, Miro Riva on a Rumi 125, Malagutti on a Ducati 98, Pietro Carissoni aboard a Rumi "125", and the FIM manager Paolo Colombo. Left, Miro Riva with ing. Bruno Guidorossi at the start of the Motogiro Toscano, where he came fourth on the October of 1954.

Milan, the 6th of April 1955, Trofeo Aldrighetti. Armando Parisio with the new "Sei Giorni" waits for the off. On the facing page, Dario Basso, first equal, photographed near Arona.

1955

ROMA-AQUILA-ROMA - Trials event
27.3.1955

Team: Mattia-Poeti-Vigorito	1st

FALKENBERG T.T. - Speed event
April 1955

Hoffmann Borje	1st 125 cm³

5th TROFEO ALDRIGHETTI - Milano - National trials event
5.4.1955

Enrico Gerosa	1st
Giuseppe Balconi	1st

95	Costanzo Daminelli	1st
	Gianpiero Zubani	1st
103	Dario Basso	1st
	Lino Scotti	1st
	Benito L'Abruzzi	1st
109	Pietro Carissoni	1st
	Aldo Zecca	1st
	Romano Crippa	1st
	Nino Pesenti	1st

VALLI FIORENTINE - Trials event
11.4.1955

Mauro Cintolesi	1st

4th TRE VALLI VARESINE - National IMF trials event
17.6.1955

Romano Crippa	1st

Romano Turotti	1st
Lino Scotti	1st
Rinaldo Caccianiga	1st

COPPA BASCHELLI - Rome
April 1955

Dario Basso	1st
Pietro Carissoni	1st
Costanzo Daminelli	1st
Team	1st

3rd GIRO MOTOCICLISTICO D'ITALIA
17.4.1955

	Pietro Carissoni	2nd 125 cm^3
	Dario Bassi	7th 125 cm^3
	Corti	8th 125 cm^3
	Costanzo Daminelli	10th 125 cm^3
281	Gianni Zonca	11th 125 cm^3
	Falegnami	12th 125 cm^3
	Vasco Rosati	13th 125 cm^3
	G. Franco Poeti	15th 125 cm^3
	Vianello	17th 125 cm^3
	Turchetti	19th 125 cm^3
	Albertini	23rd 125 cm^3
	Gianpiero Zubani	24th 125 cm^3
192	Civiero	25th 125 cm^3
	Tagli	26th 125 cm^3
	Torricelli	31st 125 cm^3
	Gualtieri	37th 125 cm^3

Overall rankings

| Pietro Carissoni | 25th overall |
| Team | 1st |

Rumi won 5 sections in the 125 class

RICCIONE-PESCARA
| Basso | 1st 125 cm^3 |
PESCARA-TARANTO
| Basso-Carissoni | 1st 125 cm^3 |

Gianni Zonca goes flat out during the 1955 Giro Motociclistico d'Italia, held on the 17th of April.

TARANTO-COSENZA
Zubani   1st 125 cm³
COSENZA-NAPOLI
Basso   1st 125 cm³
PERUGIA-BOLOGNA
Basso   1st 125 cm³

CASALE MONFERRATO - National trials event
1.5.1955

6	Pietro Carissoni	2nd
	Dario Basso	4th
19	Ennio Langinotti	19th

3rd GIRO DELLE CALABRIE - IMF national trials event
2.5.1955

Costanzo Daminelli	1st
Dario Basso	1st
Pietro Carissoni	18th
Ennio Maffezzoli	29th

Team	1st
"Motor Oil" Trophy	

DUE VALLI - Sanremo - Trials event
May 1955

Figini	1st Scooter
Lavaizza	2nd 125 Sport

In the three classes:

Team	1st

CIRCUITO DI CREMA
Italian championship - 2nd Div. speed event
7.5.1955

Gianpiero Zubano	3rd
Alfredo Falegnami	5th

Another shot of the 1955 Giro Motociclistico d'I-talia. Below, Sergio Civiero, who finished 25th. On the facing page, Gianni Zonca aboard his Rumi "Junior" at the start of a section: the photo clearly shows the central bulge in the exhaust pipe that hides the expansion box.

TROFEO ZECCHINI - Milano - Trials event
15.5.1955

Guido Fornoni	1st
Giorgio Castelli	1st
Enrico Gerosa	1st
Lino Scotti	1st

CORSA AL MARE - Rome
19.5.1955

Luigi Ciai	3rd

2nd CIRCUITO DI GALLARATE - Speed event
May 1955

Antonio Tarlizzi	3rd

6th CIRCUITO DI MONTICHIARI - Brescia - Speed event
May 1955

Enzo Mereghetti	2nd
Castelli	4th
Bianchetti	5th
Zanoletti	6th

3rd CIRCUITO DI BOVOLONE - 3rd Div. speed event
22.5.1955

Enzo Mereghetti	1st
Sardo Gerosa	2nd
Secondo Stocco	4th
Berto Semenzato	7th
Antonio Fabi	8th

PISA 12 HOURS - IMF Italian championship trials event
28.5.1955

Dario Basso	1st
Pietro Carissoni	1st
Costanzo Daminelli	1st
Ennio Longinotti	5th
Attilio Pera	5th
Ennio Maffezzoli	11th
Team	1st

CIRCUITO DI GROSSETO - Junior speed event
29.5.1955

Gianpiero Zubani	4th

CASSANO MAGNAGO - Varese - Provincial trials event
29.9.1955

Aurelio Colutta	1st

CIRCUITO DI CASTELMASSA - Speed event
29.5.1955

    Odoardo Gonzaga Guerrieri   1st

4 th MESSINA - COLLE S. RIZZO - Speed event
29.5.1955

    Pietro Smeriglio   4th

CIRCUITO PIAZZA D'ARMI
Turin - 3rd section - Junior championship speed event
5.6.1955

    Enzo Mereghetti   5th
    Eugenio Poles   6th
    Terlizzi   10th

CIRCUITO DI TORTONA - Speed event
June 1955

    Gianpiero Zubani   1st

CIRCUITO VALLELUNGA - Speed event
June 1955

    Dario Basso   1st

WARSAGE 24 HOURS - Belgium - Track speed event
June 1955

    Orinel   1st Scooter

CIRCUITO DI FABRIANO - Speed event
5.6.1955

    Mauro Cintolesi   3rd

The Circuito del Mugel-lo, 9th June 1955. Right, Mauro Cintolesi giving it his best shot; the fairing shown in the photo was later removed after it was adjudged irregular. On the facing page, Cintolesi (no. 52), who was to finish second, gets underway.

CIRCUITO DI PIAZZA D'ARMI - Turin - Regional speed event
9.6.1955

30	Davico	1st 125 Sport

CIRCUITO DEL MUGELLO - Provincial speed event
9.6.1955

52	Mauro Cintolesi	2nd
	Nardini	3rd

20th CIRCUITO DI ASTI - Speed event
June 1955

Enzo Mereghetti	1st
Bianchi	3rd
Testa	10th

5th PROVA TROFEO DRAGONI
Milano - 4th section - IMF national trials event
9-11.6.1955

52	Pietro Carissoni	3rd
	Dario Basso	5th
	Ennio Longhinotti	6th
	Costanzo Daminelli	7th
	Ennio Maffezzoli	9th
	Aldo Zecca	16th
	Team	1st

1st COPPA QUATTRO MARI - Leghorn - 2nd Div. speed event
11.6.1955

Mauro Cintolesi	2nd
Spazzolino	9th

214

Allo scattante e ammirevole "52" Mauro Antolesi caramente Ginofedi

Circuito Barberino Mugello 1955

10th MILANO-TARANTO
19.6.1955

91	Pietro Carissoni	4th 125 cm³
93	Bruno Basso	5th 125 cm³
105	Ennio Maffezzoli	6th 125 cm³
131	G. Franco Poeti	9th 125 cm³
147	Eugenio Poles	12th 125 cm³
135	Francesco La Torre	13th 125 cm³
139	Ennio Malacchi	18th 125 cm³
96	Roberto Patrignani	21st 125 cm³
	Sandro Brabetz	25th 125 cm³

Overall rankings:

Pietro Carissoni	31st overall
Dario Basso	32nd overall
Ennio Maffezzoli	35th overall

Junior class rankings:

Pietro Carissoni	1st 125 cm³
Dario Basso	2nd 125 cm³
Ennio Maffezzoli	3rd 125 cm³

10th CIRCUITO DI FROSINONE - Speed event
26.6.1955

| Franco Mancini | 2nd |
| G. Franco Spiga | 8th |

CASTELLAMMARE DI STABIA- IMF Trials event
26.6.1955

Pasquale Abate	1st
Luigi Rago	1st
Abete	1st

TROFEO CLIPPER - Milano - Trials event
June 1955

Lino Scotti	1st
Bruno Gerosa	1st
Team	1st

Left, Costanzo Daminelli and the new "Sei Giorni" with the teledraulic forks tackle the Ponte Selva bends during the Valli Bergamasche event held from the 27th to the 29th of June 1955. On the facing page, Roberto Patrignani comes in 21st in the 1955 Milano-Taranto endurance event.

8th VALLI BERGAMASCHE - IMF Italian championship trials event
27-29.6.1955

7	Dario Basso	1st
12	Ennio Longinotti	5th
21	Pietro Carissoni	5th
28	Costanzo Daminelli	8th
17	Aldo Zecca	13th
	Team	1st

CIRCUITO DI RECANATI - 3rd Div. speed event
3.7.1955

13	G. Mario Paleari	3rd
	Nino Tagli	4th
	Vasco Rosati	6th

LA LEONESSA - Brescia - 2nd Div. Sport class speed event
3.7.1955

Enzo Mereghetti	2nd
Ennio Maffezzoli	7th
Eugenio Poles	10th

BRUSSELS-BASEL-BRUSSELS
Belgium - Long distance event (1080 km)
July 1955

Chevolet-Manet	1st Scooter
Orinel	4th Scooter
Team	1st

GIRO DELLE TRE PROVINCIE
Bologna - National trials event
3.7.1955

Gianfranco Capizzi	1st
Ernesto Palmieri	1st

Some pictures from the 1955 Valli Bergamasche event. Top left, Pietro Carissoni arrives at Selvino during the night-time stage. Top right, Ennio Maffezzoli at the start. Below, Ennio Longinotti in action.

BANDIA - France - Track speed event
3.7.1955

Merz		1st Scooter class record

BOLZANO-MENDOLA - Italian hillclimb championship
10.7.1955

	Gianpiero Zubani	1st
26	Gianni Zonca	2nd
	Livio Cescati	5th
	Nino Cossu	6th
	Sergio Bertoletti	7th

CRITERIUM DELLA BRIANZA - Provincial trials event
10.7.1955

Lino Scotti	3rd
Angelo Spinelli	3rd

SWEDISH GRAND PRIX - Hedemora - track speed event
16.7.1955

| 15 | Bengt Svensson | 8th 125 Comp. |

Junior class:

| 21 | Arne Johansson | 9th 125 SS.TT |
| 22 | Hans Gustavsson | 15th 125 SS.TT |

TROFEO DELL'ORTO - Seregno - Provincial championship trials event
16.7.1955

| | Angelo Spinelli | 5th |
| | Lino Scotti | 13th |

2nd CIRCUITO DI SAN FERMO - Macerata - Speed event
16.8.1955

| | Gianpiero Zubani | 8th |
| | Mancini | 9th |

FALKENBERG T.T. - Sweden
July 1955

| | Borje Hoffmann | 1st 125 SS.TT |

DUE VALLI - San Remo - Trials event
July 1955

	Figini	1st Scooter
	Lavazza	2nd 125 Sport
	Team	1st

CIRCUITO DI VIGEVANO
2nd Div. Sport class speed event
17.7.1955

25	Gianni Zonca	1st
	Gianpiero Zubani	7th
	Enzo Mereghetti	8th

Above, the 3rd of July 1955, the Circuit of Bandia. Astride a "Formichino", the winner Merz (France) also recorded the fastest lap at 27' 49".

Right, Gianni Zonca with his Rumi "Junior" at the Circuit of Vigevano, where he won the Sport class on the 17th July 1955. Below, Ennio Maffezzoli with the "Formichino" at the finish of the Cannes-Geneva-Cannes Trophy of July 1955.

3rd CANNES-GENEVA-CANNES TROPHY - France
July 1955

Scooter class team
Carissoni-Basso-Maffezzoli   1st

7th GIRO DELLA CAMPANIA - Provincial trials event
17.7.1955

Pasquale Abate   1st

4th COPPA TOSCO-UMBRA - Firenze - trials event
17.7.1955

Attilio Pera   1st
Gori   7th

INTERNAZIONALE SU PISTA - Udine - International track speed event
10.8.1955

Dario Basso   1st 125 cm^3
Sandro Brabetz   2nd 125 cm^3

Pietro Carissoni and Dario basso at the Cannes-Geneva-Cannes. The two riders, along with Ennio Maffezzoli, formed the winning squad in the scooter class.

TRACK SPEED MEETING - Lonigo
21.8.1955

    Dario Basso   1st
    Sandro Brabetz   2nd

TROFEO CARLO MORETTI - Brescia - Trials event
August 1955

    Ennio Longinotti   1st

3rd CIRCUITO DI GRAVELLONA L. - Speed event
28.8.1955

Enzo Mereghetti   1st

CIRCUITO DI CASTELLAMARE - Speed event
28.8.1955
Enzo Rippa   1st

**TROFEO OMOBONO TENNI - Montebelluna
Speed event**
11.9.1955

    Enzo Mereghetti   3rd
    Aldo Zecca   7th

A nighttime start at Geneva for Pietro Carissoni: right, the photo shows the mechanic Silvio Forcella and the engineer Bruno Guidorossi.

222

INTERNATIONAL SIX DAYS
Gottwaldov - Czechoslovakia - IMF trials event
18.9.1955

Trophy team:

Dario Basso	125 cm³
Costanzo Daminelli	125 cm³
Pietro Carissoni	125 cm³

Vase team:

Ennio Longirotti	125 cm³
Ennio Maffezzoli	125 cm³

The entire Italian team retired during the second day following the death of Serafino Dietrich.

GIRO DELLE ALPI - Austria - Trials event
September 1955

Raimond Voll	1st 125 cm³

METTET - Belgium - Track speed event
September 1955

Ransell	1st 125 Comp.

TRENTO-MONTE BONDONE - Hillclimb
18.9.1955

Gianni Zonca	1st
Gianpiero Zubani	2nd
Aldo Zecca	3rd
Nicola Bovolenta	9th
Gherardo Colombi	10th
Livio Cescatti	11th

GIRO DEI MONTI PRENESTINI - Rome - Provincial trials event
2.10.1955

Luigi Ciai	1st

Sergio Mattia	3rd
G. Franco Poeti	6th

SORRENTO-SANT'AGATA - Hillclimb
2.10.1955

Vincenzo Rippa	2nd
Edoardo Rippa	5th

FLYING KILOMETRE - Monza Autodrome
6.10.1955

Attilio Damiani	12th
Longo	15th
Tenconi	16th
Castelli	17th
Scarcella	19th

CAMPIONATO PROVINCIALE F.M.I. - Verona - Trials event
October 1955

Pellegrini	1st
Bassaggio	1st

September 1955, the International Six Days Trial circus hits Czechoslovakia. The International Trophy team; from the left, team manager Carletto Merlo, Costanzo Daminelli on a Rumi, Benzoni on a Laverda, Domenico Fenocchio on a Gilera, Dario Basso and Pietro Carissoni, both riding a Rumi.

223

Pietro Carissoni's work bike at the start of the 1955 International Six Days Trial event. The rider's name is visible on the steering head. On the facing page, Silvano Forcella, the rider-mechanic who came 1st equal in the Trofeo Orobico, held in the April of 1956.

2nd TROFEO REDA - Bergamo - Grasstrack speed event
23.10.1955

Dario Basso	1st 125 cm³
Piero Carissoni	2nd 125 cm³
Attilio Damiani	4th 125 cm³
Aldo Zecca	5th 125 cm³
Lino Cornago	8th 125 cm³
Gianni Zonca	2nd 175 cm³

TROFEO DI REGOLARITÀ F.M.I.
Gravellona L. - Trials event
30.10.1955

Angelo Spinelli	3rd
Enrico Gerosa	15th
Attilio Damiani	16th

COPPA A. GRANA - Regional trials championship final

6.11.1955

Sergio Mattia	3rd
Luigi Ciai	3rd

At the end of the 1955 season:

Gianpiero Zubani	riding a Rumi, won the "Casco Tricolore", an Italian title awarded for Junior class road racing.
Gianni Zonca	riding Rumi, won the "Casco Tricolore", an Italian title for Senior class hillclimb competition.
Ferruccio Delle Fusine	riding a Rumi, won the 125 class of the Venezuelan national speed championship.
Moto Rumi	won the Italian trials constructors' championship with: Dario Basso, Pietro Carissoni, and Costanzo Daminelli.

224

1956

SALITA DELLE TORRICELLE - Verona - Hillclimb
16.3.1956

Sardo Gerosa	5th
Enzo Mereghetti	6th
Attilio Damiani	7th
Giovanni Tosi	9th

6th TROFEO OROBICO - Bergamo - National trials event
6.4.1956

	Enrico Vanoncini	1st
	Armando Parisio	1st
	Domenico Fenocchio	1st
64	Silvano Forcella	1st
	Team	1st

CRITERIUM NATIONAL - Monthléry Autodrome - France
15.4.1956

Fréze	1st Scooter
Roby	1st 125 cm³

4th GIRO MOTOCICLISTICO D'ITALIA - Motogiro
19.4.1956

Section winners
1st section:
Enrico Vanoncini	125 M.S.D.

2nd section:
Enrico Vanoncini	125 M.S.D.

3rd section:
Vasco Rosati	125 M.S.D.

November 1956, Ferruccio Delle Fusine won the Venezuelan Championship for the third time running. The handsome aluminium "dustbin" fairing was built by his father Giuseppe, an ex-racer, over a specially modified second series "Gobbetto" frame.

4th section:	
Vasco Rosati	125 M.S.D.
5th section:	
Vasco Rosati	125 M.S.D.
6th section:	
Vasco Rosati	125 M.S.D.
7th section:	
Vasco Rosati	125 M.S.D.
8th section:	
Vasco Rosati	125 M.S.D.

Overall rankings:

	Enzo Torreggiani	9th 125 Sport
237	Gino Padovan	10th 125 Sport
241	Roberto Patrignani	13 125 Sport
	Attilio Di Fino	14th 125 Sport
	Vasco Rosati	1st 125 M.S.D.
53	Enrico Vanoncini	2nd 125 Sport

CIRCUITO DI ASOLA - Provincial-Regional speed event
1.5.1956

Provincial championship:

Enzo Torreggiani	2nd 125 cm³

Regional championship:

Enzo Mereghetti	3rd 125 cm³
Franco Moriggia	6th 125 cm³
Andrea Zucchi	7th 125 cm³
Attilio Damiani	8th 125 cm³
Aldo Zecca	9th 125 cm³
Sardo Gerosa	10th 125 cm³

4th ROMA-OSTIA - Speed event
May 1956

Alvaro Mucci	3rd

CIRCUITO DI LUGO - Ravenna - Speed event
10.5.1956

Eugenio Poles	7th

CIRCUITO DI CAMERINO - Junior speed event
10.5.1956

Grassetti	7th
Moretti	11th

TUBBERGEN - Holland - Speed event
27.5.1956

Van Bockel	1st 125 cm³

THE BOL D'OR 24 HOURS - Monthléry - France - Speed event
3.6.1956

Cambis-Dital	1st Scooter

DORIA-CRETO - National hillclimb
3.6.1956

Alfredo Falegnami	2nd 125 Sport
Attilio Damiani	5th 125 Sport
Aldo Zecca	7th 125 Sport
Franco Bertolotti	8th 125 Sport
Giovanni Albalustri	9th 125 Sport

PIANA DI ROVIGO - Speed
3.6.1956

Sandro Brabetz	2nd 125 cm^3

STEZZANO-BERGAMO - Gymkhana - 2nd round Prov. champ.
3.6.1956

Giovanni Gritti	2nd

11th MILANO-TARANTO
10.6.1956

	Morlacchi	6th 125 M.S.D.
104	Roberto Patrignani	7th

Roberto Patrignani and his Rumi "Junior" during the 11th Milano-Taranto endurance event of the 10th June 1956.

Right, Roberto Patrignano arriving at the promenade in Taranto. Below right, Gosta Karlson on the Rumi "Junior" with which he took third place in the Swedish GP at Hedemora on the 14th July 1956.

CASTELLETTO D'ORBA - Gymkhana - 2nd round Pr. champ. 2nd round Prov. champ.
10.6.1956

Osvaldo Raitieri	2nd
Renzo Marchelli	4th

TROFEO DELL'ORTO
June 1956

Angelo Spinelli	13th

CIRCUITO DI MACERATA - 2nd Div. speed event
17.6.1956

Grassetti	8th
Vasco Rosati	11th

ARICCIA-MONTE CALVO - hillclimb
June 1956

Alvaro Mucci	5th

Two shots of the 1956 Valli Bergamasche event. Above, Gianni Zonca, who came 9th. Bottom left, Angelo Spinelli during the second day of competition; he came 23rd.

9th VALLI BERGAMASCHE - Bergamo - 4th round IMF National trials event
1.7.1956

22	Gianni Zonca	9th
21	Angelo Spinelli	23rd

1st TROFEO GHIRLANDINA - Modena - 3rd Div. speed event
10.7.1956

Aldo Tosini	6th Cadetti
Sergio Mazzoni	8th
Walter Scarcella	9th

SWEDISH GRAND PRIX - Hedemora - track speed event
14.7.1956

45	Gösta Karlsson	3rd 125 Comp.

32	Olof Wallin	6th 125 SS.TT
33	Ingemar Blomquist	8th 125 cm³
54	Karl Jansson	9th 125 cm³
48	Leif Hedman	10th 125 cm³
38	Arne Johansson	11th 125 Comp.
52	Lennart Karlsson	12th 125 cm³
31	Hans Gustavsson	13th 125 cm³
35	Ivan Svensson	14th 125 cm³
46	Lars Sjostrom	15th 125 cm³
41	Stig Tedesater	16th 125 cm³
49	Arne Nordstrom	18th 125 cm³

VASTKUSTOLOPPET - Sweden - Junior class speed event
July 1956

| Gosta Karlsson | 3rd 125 cm³ |

UDINE - Track speed event
15.7.1956

| Luciano Vianello | 3rd |
| Sandro Brabetz | 4th |

1st TROFEO REDA DEZZO
Presolana - Bergamo - Hillclimb
22.7.1956

23	Lino Cornago	13th
21	G. Franco Saini	14th
35	Ruggero Gianoli	19th
25	Silvano Forcella	20th
24	Giuseppe Panseri	25th
33	Giorgio Castelli	26th

FOLLONICA - Track speed event
22.7.1956

| Luciano Petri | 3rd |

| Mario Papi | 4th |
| Francesco Gigli | 5th |

TAVERNUZZE-IMPRUNETA - Hillclimb
29.7.1956

Aldo Tosini	3rd
Alfredo Falegnami	5th
Franco Manucci	10th

13th COPPA DELLA CONSUMA - Hillclimb
5.8.1956

| Aldo Tosini | 4th |
| Guglielmo Magrini | 6th |

CIRCUITO DI CINGOLI - Speed event
August 1956

| Silvio Grassetti | 7th |
| Franco Manucci | 9th |

3rd CIRCUITO DI CUNEO - Speed event
12.8.1956

L. Mannino	9th
A. Terlizzi	10th
C. Cucchi	11th
G. Benso	12th

MONTAGNANA - Vicenza - National track speed event
16.8.1956

| Giuseppe Filira | 1st |
| Sardo Gerosa | 2nd |

14th October 1956, Vermicino-Rocca di Papa: Gianni Perrone, who won aboard a Rumi "Sport". The beginning of a section during the 5th Motogiro, held between the 9th and 18th of April 1957.

TRENTO-MONTE BONDONE - Hillclimb
19.8.1956

Attilio Damiani	2nd
Menegol	3rd

FOLLONICA - National speed event
August 1956

Mario Barbieri	3rd

4th CIRCUITO DI CASTELLAMARE DI STABIA
National speed event
August 1956

Padolecchia	6th
Caramiello	7th

COPPA G. MORETTI - Vicenza - Speed event
2.9.1956

Mannucci	7th

PISTA DI MALO - Vicenza - Speed event
2.9.1956

Sandro Brabetz	4th
Antonio Fabi	5th

THE TRIPOLI TROPHY - North Africa - Trials event
2.9.1956

Consolandi	1st

SORRENTO-SANT'AGATA - Hillclimb
23.9.1956

Silvio Jannuzzi	1st
Vincenzo Rippa	2nd

CIRCUITO CAMPO DI MARTE - Florence - Road race
30.9.1956

Vasco Rosati	7th

MODENA AUTODROME - 3rd Div. speed event
30.9.1956

Lino Cornago	6th 125 cm^3
Giuseppe Panseri	8th 125 cm^3

CIRCUITO ARCO DI ADRIANO - Junior class speed event
7.10.1956

Fancinelli	5th
Caramiello	6th

MODENA AUTODROME - Junior championship final
14.10.1956

Vasco Rosati	17th 125 cm^3

TROFEO MORETTI - Brescia - Trials event
14.10.1956

Lino Cornago	7th
Giuseppe Panseri	8th
Enrico Vanoncini	8th

26th VERMICINO-ROCCA DI PAPA - Hillclimb
14.10.1956

Gianni Perrone	1st 125 M.S.D.

2nd GIRO DELLA TOSCANA - Trials event
21.10.1956

Aldo Tosini	4th

TROFEO F.M.I. - Gravellona L. - Trials event
28.10.1956

Angelo Spinelli	1st
Lino Cornago	1st

At the end of the 1956 Season:

Ferruccio Delle Fusine	riding a Rumi, won the 125 cm^3 class of the Venezuelan National Speed Championships.

1957

COTE LAPIZE-MONTHLÉRY - France - Hillclimb
March 1957

| Cambis | 1st 125 Sport |
| Cambis | 1st production 125 |

SALITA DELLE TORRICELLE
Verona - Junior speed event
19.3.1957

| Sardo Gerosa | 1st |
| Bazzini | 5th |

TROFEO CADETTI - Modena - speed event
7.4.1957

| Luciano Spinello | 3rd 125 cm³ |

5th GIRO MOTOCICLISTICO D'ITALIA - Motogiro
9-18.4.1957

Overall rankings

77	Gianni Zonca	4th 125 cm³ F.3
44	Lino Cornago	9th 125 cm³ F.3
57	Roberto Patrignani	13th 125 cm³ F.3
65	Luciano Vianello	194th 125 cm³ F.3

TROFEO DELL'ORTO - Seregno - Provincial trials event
14.4.1957

| Angelo Spinelli | 5th |
| Lino Scotti | 12th |

A section start during the 5th Motogiro, which was held from the 9th to the 18 of April 1957.

Above, the 1957 Moto-giro: Gianni Zonca (no. 77) amid a group of competitors. Right, autumn 1957, the "Formichinos" ridden by Cambis and Etienne, winners of the 29th Bol D'Or at Montl-léry, on display at the Paris Show.

TROFEO ESSO - Piacenza - National trials event
22.4.1957

Angelo Spinelli	30th

DORIA-CRETO - Hillclimb
22.4.1957

Franco Bertirotti	3rd 125 F.2
Flavio Grana	4th
Ezio Cavanna	6th

CIRCUITO DI RICCIONE - Speed event
22.4.1957

Mannucci	8th

THE MONTHLÉRY TWO HOURS
France - Track speed event
May 1957

Cambis	2nd 125 Sport
Joubert	3rd production 125

TROFEO CADETTI F.M.I. - Modena - speed event
5.5.1957

26	Romano Bazzini	1st 125 cm^3

5th CORSA AL MARE - Roma/Ostia - Speed event
5.5.1957

Elio Sporazzini	1st

Lino Cornago and Gianni Zonca at the Reda Trophy (Bergamo) on the 12th of May 1957. The pair came fourth and first respectively; between them, in the overalls, Silvano Forcella.

CIRCUITO DI ASOLA - Speed event
10.5.1957

Santini	4th
Bruno Gerosa	5th
Roberto Patrignani	6th
Cremonini	7th

TROFEO REDA - Bergamo - Speed event
12.5.1957

74	Gianni Zonca	1st 125 cm^3
	Ruggero Gianoli	3rd
80	Lino Cornago	4th
	Luciano Spinello	6th

CIRCUITO DI CAMERINO - Speed event
19.5.1957

Sauro Banchetti	7th

29th BOL D'OR 24 HOURS - Monthléry - Monthléry - France
June 1957

Cambis-Etienne (1,884.461 km, average 78.519 km/h)	1st Scooter
Leguellec/Christophe	2nd Scooter

VALLI FIORENTINE - Trials
2.6.1957

Aldo Tosini	6th
Romano Cassi	8th

Right, Giuseppe Panseri during the Trofeo Reda. Far right, the Ljubelj-Bergrennen (Austria) hillclimb held in August 1957; neither the name nor the result obtained by the rider on the Rumi "Scoiattolo" is known.

TROFEO ZENIT - Melegnano - Provincial trials event
2.6.1957

Giorgio Castelli	22nd	

LONIGO - International track event
9.6.1957

Sardo Gerosa	2nd 125 cm³	
Sandro Brabetz	3rd 125 cm³	

VALLI BERGAMASCHE - Bergamo - National trials event
28-30.6.1957

25	Angelo Spinelli	5th

CIRCUITO DI GALLARATE - Junior championship speed event
2.8.1957

Gianni Zonca	10th	

8th TRENTO-MONTE BONDONE - Hillclimb
4.8.1957

Attilio Damiani	3rd	
Silvano Forcella	6th	

4th FASANO-SELVA - Speed event
11.8.1957

Caramiello	6th	

Two snaps taken on the 10th November 1957 during the seventh Trofeo Orobico. Near left, Gianni Perini, who did not finish. Far left, Angelo Spinelli, who came fifth.

FOLLONICA - Track speed event
15.8.1957

    Sardo Gerosa   3rd

1st VIANO-BISSA - Reggio Emilia - Hillclimb
August 1957

    Biazzini   7th

PONTEDECIMO-GIOVI - Hillclimb
7.9.1957

    Giorgio Castelli   6th
    Luigi Arcoletti   12th

    Gino Albalustri   16th
    Enzo Cavanna   17th

TROFEO F.M.I. - Seregno - National trials - last section
September 1957

    Angelo Spinelli   1st

3rd MOTOGIRO DELLA TOSCANA - Provincial trials event
18.9.1957

    Aldo Tosini   2nd

7th TROFEO OROBICO - Bergamo - Trials event
10.11.1957

    Angelo Spinelli   5th

1958

COTE LAPIZE-MONTHLÉRY - France - Hillclimb
March 1958

Cambis	1st Scooter Comp.
Caeckebecke	1st Scooter Sport
Tano	1st Standard Scooter

VALLELUNGA - Rome - Speed event
16.3.1958

Fausto Amicucci	2nd 125 F.2

TROFEO REDA - Bergamo - Circuit trials event
23.3.1958

Romano Crippa	1st
Angelo Spinelli	1st
Lino Cornago	1st
Gianni Zonca	16th
Carlo Moscheni	22nd
G. Franco Palazzoli	22nd

TRIALS CHAMPIONSHIPS - Florence
April 1958

Group C:	
Carlo Moscheni	1st
Lino Cornago	2nd
Gianni Zonca	3rd
Team	3rd

TROFEO EDOARDO BIANCHI
Varese - Italian trials championships event
20.4.1958

Carlo Moscheni	8th

The Trofeo Reda of the 23rd March 1958. Left, Gian Franco Palazzoli, who came 22nd. On the facing page, Romano Crippa, who came 1st equal.

CIRCUITO DEL MARE - Pesaro - Senior speed event
20.4.1958

Gianni Zonca	1st
Lino Cornago	4th

CIRCUITO DI MODENA - 2nd Div. speed event
26.4.1958

Luciano Spinello	4th
Angelo Orsenigo	5th
Silvano Forcella	6th
Romano Crippa	7th
Franco Arturi	13th
Claudio Candutti	14th

CIRCUITO DI BUSTO ARSIZIO
Constructors' championship speed event
1.5.1958

Gianni Zonca	4th
Lino Cornago	6th
Angelo Orsenigo	8th
Vasco Rosati	9th

16th DORIA-CRETO - Hillclimb
May 1958

Flavio Grana	2nd
Franco Arturi	4th

Two pictures from the Reda Trophy. Above, Gianni Zonca, who came 16th, gets stuck in. Bottom right, Carlo Moscheni fords a stream: he came 22nd.

3rd ROUND OF THE ITALIAN CHAMPIONSHIP
Reggio Emilia
8.5.1958

Carlo Moscheni	1st
Angelo Spinelli	1st

MONTHLÉRY - France - Speed event
8.5.1958

Bourles	1st 125 Sport

10th VALLI BERGAMASCHE - National trials event
31-2.5-6.1958

Carlo Moscheni	13th

Carlo Moscheni during the 1958 Valli Bergamasche event, where he came 13th.

Three photos from the Valli Bergamasche, held from the 31st of May to the 2nd of June. Top and centre, Gianni Perini. Bottom, Eugenio Saini.

THE BOL D'OR 24 HOURS - Monthléry - France - Speed event
June 1958

    Foidelli-Bois   1st Scooter
(a new record at an average of 87.327 km/h)

    Bourles-Talbot   1st 125 Sport

TROFEO BONESCHI - Melegnano - National trials event
June 1958

    Angelo Spinelli   1st
    Carlo Moscheni   1st
    The "Fiamme d'Oro" team:
    Moscheni-Spinelli-Vergani   1st

ZOLDER - Belgium - Speed event
June 1958

    Nibou   1st 125 Sport

CIRCUITO DI PESARO - Hillclimb
June 1958

    Vasco Rosati   1st 125 F.2

APPIANO-PASSO MENDOLA - National hillclimb
8.6.1958

    Gianni Zonca   1st 125 F.3
    Lino Cornago   4th 125 F.3
    Enzo Mereghetti   5th 125 F.3

CIRCUITO DI ALESSANDRIA
2nd Div. championship - Junior speed event
8.6.1958

    Luciano Spinello   2nd 125 F.3

Silvano Forcella	4th
Angelo Orsenigo	6th
Claudio Candutti	8th
Giovanni Varchi	10th

PONTEDECIMO-BOCCHETTA - Hillclimb
8.6.1958

| Franco Arturi | 2nd |
| Flavio Grana | 3rd |

TROFEO L. TADINI - National trials event
15.6.1958

| Angelo Spinelli | 15th |

CASTELL'ARQUATO-VERNASCA - Hillclimb
22.6.1958

| Tersilio Censi | 3rd |
| Giovanni Pollenghi | 4th |

CIRCUITO DI CUNEO - Senior speed event
22.6.1958

Gianni Zonca	1st
Lino Cornago	4th
Luciano Spinello	6th
Bona	9th

PONTEDECIMO-GIOVI - Hillclimb
29.6.1958

Sergio Amadei	2nd
Flavio Grana	3rd
Claudio Candutti	4th
Pietro Rellecati	5th
Italo Piana	6th
Alfredo Gatta	7th

COPPA E. BIANCHI - Varese - Trials event
29.6.1958

| Carlo Moscheni | 16th |
| Angelo Spinelli | 17th |
The "Fiamme Oro" team:
Spinelli-Moscheni-Vergani

CIRCUITO DI CAMERINO - Drivers 'Constructors' speed event
6.7.1958

Gianni Zonca	4th
Lino Cornago	8th
Roberto Patrignani	9th

9th TRENTO-MONTE BONDONE - Hillclimb
6.7.1958

| Silvano Forcella | 3rd |
| Ruggero Gianoli | 5th |

THE ITALIAN TRIALS CHAMPIONSHIPS
Piacenza - Final section
13.7.1958

| Angelo Spinelli | 1st 125 cm^3 |

BOLOGNA-S. LUCA - Hillclimb
13.7.1958

| Franco Mannucci | 7th |

GARESSIO-SAN BERNARDO - Aosta - Hillclimb
July 1958

| Franco Arturi | 1st |

COLLEFERRO-SEGNI - Hillclimb
20.7.1958

Amicucci	3rd 125 F.2

VOLTRI-TURCHINO - Hillclimb
20.7.1958

Franco Arturi	3rd
Flavio Grana	5th
Angelo Spinelli	7th

CIRCUITO LAGHI GANZIRRI - Messina - Speed event
27.7.1958

Silvano Rinaldi	9th

AOSTA-PEROULAZ - F.3 hillclimb
27.7.1958

Lino Cornago	1st 125 F.3
Romano Crippa	2nd 125 F.3
Silvano Forcella	3rd 125 F.3
Italo Piana	4th 125 F.3

CIRCUITO DI ABBADIA - Junior hillclimb
3.8.1958

Angelo Spinelli	5th

COPPA VILLA ALMÉ - Provincial trials event
3.8.1958

Romano Crippa	1st
Gianni Perini	22nd

CIRCUITO DI SAN FERMO - Constructors' speed championships
17.8.1958

Silvano Rinaldi	5th 125 cm³
Roberto Patrignani	10th 125 cm³

125 Junior class:

Gianni Zonca	6th
Roberto Patrignani	7th
Lino Cornago	10th

VARESE-CAMPO DEI FIORI - Hillclimb
29.8.1958

Angelo Orsenigo	6th
Alfredo Gabba	7th
Italo Piana	9th

REGOLARITÀ DI VERTOVA - Bergamo - Provincial trials
31.8.1958

24	Eugenio Saini	1st
26	Gianni Perini	1st

TESERO-STAVA-PAMPEAGO - National hillclimb championships
31.8.1958

Lino Cornago	1st
Silvano Forcella	4th

CESAREO-MONTECOMPATRI - National hillclimb championships
31.8.1958

Fausto Amicucci	4th
Natale Baranello	5th

VALLELUNGA - Italian 2nd Div. championships
7.9.1958

Natale Baranello	6th 125 F.3

The 31st August 1958: the Vertova trials event. Eugenio Saini on his way to victory.

PONTEDECIMO-GIOVI - Hillclimb
September 1958

Franco Arturi	4th
Flavio Grana	5th
Pietro Relecati	7th

THE MODENA AUTODROME - Trofeo Cadetti
19.9.1958

Silvano Forcella	7th
Angelo Orsenigo	9th
Claudio Candutti	12th
Giovanni Varchi	13th

5th COPPA CITTÀ DI MORCIANO - Forlì - Speed event
September 1958

Luciano Spinello	5th

RECCO-USCIO - Hillclimb
1.10.1958

Luciano Bindini	8th 125 F.3

TRIESTE-OPICINA - F.3 Hillclimb
October 1958

Lino Cornago	1st

FRASCATI-ROCCA DI PAPA - Hillclimb
October 1958

    Natale Baranello   5th 125 F.3

MONTHLÉRY - FRANCE - Track speed event
October 1958

Cambis	1st Scooter Comp.
Caeckebecke	1st Scooter Sport
Leclainche	1st Scooter

TAVERNUZZE-IMPRUNETA - Florence - F.2 hillclimb
15.10.1958

    Flavio Grana   1st

At the end of the 1958 season:

Gianni Zonca	riding a Rumi, took 5th place in the 125 cm^3 class of the Italian Junior Speed Championship.
Roberto Patrignani	riding a Rumi, took 6th place in the 125 cm^3 class of the Italian Junior Speed Championship.
Moto Rumi	came 4th in the Italian Constructors' Championship

1959

COTE LAPIZE-MONTHLÉRY - France - Hillclimb
8.3.1959

    Caeckebecke   1st 125 Sport Scooter
(average speed: 69.388 km/h)

Leguellec   1st 175 Comp. Scooter

CIRCUITO DI MODENA - Trofeo Cadetti - speed event
March 1959

Luciano Spinello	4th
Luciani Bindini	8th
Angelo Orsenigo	9th
Silvano Forcella	10th
Giuseppe Panseri	12th

DORIA-CRETO - Genoa - Hillclimb
30.3.1959

    Giovanni Pizzorno   1st 125 Sport

CIRCUITO DI CESENATICO- 2nd Div. speed event
25.4.1959

    Luciano Spinello   7th

ROMA-OSTIA - F.3 Speed event
1.5.1959

Ferdinando Pierotti	4th
Natale Baranello	6th

TROFEO ASCIAMPRENER - Milano - Criterium trials
3.5.1959

    Crugnola   1st

MONZA AUTODROME - Trofeo Cadetti - speed event

Angelo Spinelli	8th 125 cm^3
Angelo Orsenigo	11th 125 cm^3
Silvano Forcella	15th 125 cm^3

Giovanni Varchi	16th 125 cm^3
Visenzi	17th 125 cm^3
Battista Ricci	18th 125 cm^3
Alfredo Gabba	19th 125 cm^3
Giovanni Maranesi	21st 125 cm^3
Sandro Casalini	22nd 125 cm^3

CIRCUITO DI CAMERINO - F.2 speed event
24.5.1959

| Luciano Spinello | 3rd |
| Angelo Orsenigo | 4th |

VOLTRI-TURCHINO - Hillclimb
24.5.1959

Battista Ricci	1st 125 F.2
Guido Ricchiardone	2nd 125 F.2
Aldo Cresta	4th 125 F.2
Flavio Grana	5th 125 F.2
Franco Arturi	1st 125 Sport
Alfredo Gabba	3rd 125 Sport
Sandro Casalini	4th 125 Sport

MONTHLÉRY TWO HOURS - France - speed event
May 1959

| Constans | 1st 125 Sport |

2nd BOLOGNA-SAN LUCA - Hillclimb
May 1959

| Luciano Bindini | 8th 125 F.3 |
| Giovanni Maranesi | 11th |

THE BOL D'OR 24 HOURS
Monthléry - France - Endurance-speed event
6-7.6.1959

| Boules-Talbot | 1st 125 Comp. |

(2,106 kms at an average of 87.784 km/h)

PISTA PIANA - Rovigo - Speed event
7.6.1959

| Sardo Gerosa | 2nd |

CITTÀ DI TRADATE - Trials event
14.6.1959

| Nino Pesenti | 1st |
| Sergio Mangano | 32nd |

3rd VIANO-BAISO - Hillclimb
28.6.1959

| Franco Arturi | 1st 125 F.2 |
| Luciano Spinello | 4th 125 Sport |

GARESSIO-SAN BERNARDO - Aosta - Hillclimb
June 1959

| Franco Arturi | 1st 125 Sport |

ARICCIA-MADONNA DEL TUFO - Hillclimb
28.6.1959

| Franco Trabalzini | 2nd 125 Sport |
| Ferdinando Pierotti | 5th 125 Sport |

RAPALLO-MONTALLEGRO - Hillclimb
June 1959

| Franco Arturi | 1st 125 Sport |
| Angelo Orsenigo | 3rd 125 Sport |

Luciano Spinello	5th 125 Sport
Alfredo Gabba	7th 125 Sport
Guido Ricchiardone	2nd 125 F.2
Silvio Grana	3rd 125 F.2
Battista Ricci	4th 125 F.2
Franco Pastorino	8th 125 F.2
Luciano Brizzolari	9th 125 F.2
Aldo Cresta	10th 125 F.2

TRENTO-MONTE BONDONE - Hillclimb
10.7.1959

| Silvano Forcella | 1st 125 F.3 |
| Luciano Spinello | 3rd 125 F.3 |

THE SHELL TROPHY - Cremona - Provincial trials event
24.7.1959

| G. Franco Tacchini | 1st |

FASANO-SELVA - Hillclimb
1.8.1959

| Franco Arturi | 4th 125 F.2 |

CASTELL'ARQUATO-VERNASCA - Hillclimb
23.8.1959

| Silvano Cavini | 8th 125 F.2 |
| Franco Arturi | 1st 125 Sport |

FORNACI DI BARGA - Hillclimb
23.8.1959

Guido Ricchiardone	2nd 125 F.2
Maffucci	4th 125 F.2
Deprato	3rd 125 Sport
Battista Ricci	4th 125 Sport

12th VARESE-CAMPO DEI FIORI - Hillclimb
30.8.1959

Luciano Spinello	1st
Angelo Orsenigo	2nd
Silvano Forcella	3rd

12th PONTEDECIMO-GIOVI - Hillclimb
13.9.1959

Franco Arturi	1st 125 F.2
Battista Ricci	3rd 125 F.2
Franco Pastorino	6th 125 F.2
Guido Ricchiardone	7th 125 F.2
Luciano Spinello	1st 125 Sport
Silvano Forcella	2nd 125 Sport
Tonino Nesci	3rd 125 Sport
Alfredo Gabba	4th 125 Sport

SASSI-SUPERGA
26.9.1959

Luciano Spinello	1st 125 Sport
Silvano Forcella	2nd 125 Sport
Angelo Orsenigo	3rd 125 Sport
Guido Ricchiardone	4th 125 Sport
Sandro Casalini	5th 125 Sport
Franco Arturi	5th 125 F.2
Raspino	7th

ROCCA DI PAPA - Hillclimb
2.10.1959

Luciano Spinello	2nd 125 Sport
Silvano Forcella	3rd 125 Sport
Pierotti	4th 125 Sport

PASSO DELLA SOMMA - Terni - Hillclimb
11.10.1959

Silvano Forcella	1st 125 F.2
Luciano Spinello	2nd 125 Sport
Sergio Moscato	3rd 125 Sport

RECCO-USCIO Hillclimb
18.10.1959

Battista Ricci	1st 125 Sport
Silvano Forcella	2nd 125 Sport
Nicola Sottile	3rd 125 Sport
Sandro Casalini	4th 125 Sport
Tonino Nesci	5th 125 Sport
Franco Arturi	4th 125 F.2
Giuseppe Ricci	7th 125 F.2
Franco Pastorino	8th 125 F.2

WATKINS GLEN - USA - 100 miles track event
November 1959

| Boier | 1st 125 Comp. |

At the end of the 1959 season:

Luciano Spinello	riding a Rumi, won the 125 Sport class of the Italian Hillclimb Championships.
Silvano Forcella	was runner-up aboard a Rumi.
Angelo Orsenigo	came third also aboard a Rumi.
Franco Arturi	riding a Rumi, took second place in the 125cm^3 class of the Italian Hillclimb Championship.
Luciano Spinello	came 7th in the Italian Junior Championships.

1960

COTE LAPIZE- MONTHLÉRY - France - Hillclimb
March 1960

| Offenstad | 1st 125 Sport |

FRASCATI-TUSCOLO
8.4.1960

| Balducci | 3rd 125 Sport |

DORIA-CRETO - Hillclimb
15.4.1960

Luciano Spinello	1st 125 Sport
Franco Arturi	2nd 125 Sport
Battista Ricci	3rd 125 Sport
Alfredo Gabba	4th 125 Sport

THE MONTHLÉRY TWO HOURS - France - Speed event
7.5.1960

| Christoffe | 1st 125 Sport |

BRACCIALE D'ORO
Monza Autodrome - 2nd Div. speed event
8.5.1960

Battista Ricci	3rd 125 cm^3
Guido Ricchiardone	3rd 125 cm^3
Giuseppe Ricci	6th 125 cm^3
Sottile	7th 125 cm^3
Di Ceglie	8th 125 cm^3

SASSI-SUPERGA - Hillclimb
8.5.1960

Franco Arturi's 175 cm^3 Rumi Special could not take part in the Formula 2 class (for 175 cm^3 bikes) in the 1960 Sassi-Superga event as it was deemed irregular by the Federation scrutineers. As the photo clearly shows, the frame had been modified to house the V 125 and 175 twin engines designed by Umberto Ottolenghi.

23	Gilberto Ricci	3rd 125 F.2
22	Franco Arturi	8th 125 F.2
36	Battista Perego	2nd 125 Sport
34	Silvano Forcella	5th 125 Sport
35	Alfredo Gabba	6th 125 Sport
49	Gianni Zonca	9th 175 F.2

Franco Arturi	7th 175 F.2
Franco Arturi	1st 125 Sport
Battista Ricci	2nd 125 Sport
Luciano Spinello	4th 125 Sport
Battista Perego	5th 125 Sport
Silvano Forcella	6th 125 Sport
Agostino Incao	7th 125 Sport
Mirko Pennacchio	9th 125 Sport

PONTEDECIMO-BOCCHETTA - Hillclimb
May 1960

Gilberto Ricci	2nd 125 F.2
Giuseppe Visenzi	4th 125 F.2
Lino Cornago	6th 125 F.2
Giuseppe Ricci	8th 125 F.2
Aldo Cresta	9th 125 F.2
Gianni Zonca	3rd 175 F.2

SAVONA-CADIBONA - Hillclimb
12.6.1960

Franco Arturi	1st 125 F.3
Elio Monti	2nd 125 F.3
Battista Renzi	3rd 125 F.3
Orlando Mion	2nd 125 F.2
Giuseppe Rizzi	6th 125 F.2

1st TROFEO GO-KART - Cesena - National speed event
26.6.1960

Walter Tassinari	1st Dogi Rumi
Giuseppe Bandini	2nd Dogi Rumi
Renato Lucchini	7th Dogi Rumi

THE BOL D'OR 24 HOURS - Monthléry - France
Endurance-speed event
June 1960

Foidelli-Bourles	1st 125 Comp.

STRETTURA-PASSO DELLA SOMMA - Speed event
June 1960

Gilberto Ricci	3rd 125 F.2
Luciano Spinello	4th 125 F.3

TRENTO-MONTE BONDONE - Hillclimb
26.6.1960

Luciano Spinello	1st 125 Sport
Battista Perego	4th 125 Sport
Franco Arturi	5th 125 Sport
Silvano Forcella	6th 125 Sport
Gilberto Ricci	1st 125 F.2

VOLTRI-TURCHINO - Hillclimb
3.7.1960

Franco Arturi	1st 125 Sport
Gilberto Ricci	2nd 125 Sport
Angelo Orsenigo	4th 125 Sport
Gilberto Ricci	2nd 125 F.2
Giuseppe Ricci	3rd 125 F.2
Aldo Cresta	4th 125 F.2
Tonino Nesci	5th 125 F.2

GARESSIO-SAN BERNARDO - Hillclimb
3.7.1960

Gilberto Ricci	2nd 125 F.2
Elio Monti	3rd 125 F.2
Franco Arturi	2nd 125 Sport
Luciano Spinello	2nd 125 Sport
Sottile	4th 125 Sport
Giuseppe Ricci	5th 125 Sport

CERNOBBIO-BISBINO-Como - Hillclimb
10.7.1960

Giuseppe Ricci	2nd 125 F.2
Aldo Cresta	2nd 125 F.3
Franco Arturi	3rd 125 F.3
Gilberto Ricci	4th 125 F.3
Angelo Orsenigo	5th 125 F.3

TROFEO LUCIANO DALL'ARA - Bergamo
Provincial trials event
17.7.1960

Enzo Moscheni	16th
Franco Madaschi	29th

AOSTA-PEROULAZ - Hillclimb
July 1960

Luciano Spinello	1st 125 Sport
Angelo Orsenigo	3rd 125 Sport

PONTEDECIMO-GIOVI - Hillclimb
4.9.1960

Gilberto Ricci	1st 125 F.3
Franco Arturi	2nd 125 F.3
Sandro Casalini	5th 125 F.3

Orlando Mion	2nd 125 F.2
Gilberto Ricci	3rd 125 F.2
Giuseppe Ricci	4th 125 F.2

THE CONSTRUCTORS' CHAMPIONSHIP
Monza - Autodrome - Speed event
9.9.1960

| Silvano Forcella | 22nd 125 cm^3 |
| Gilberto Ricci | 23rd 125 cm^3 |

BRACCIALE D'ORO - Monza Autodrome
2nd Div. speed event
9.10.1960

| Guido Ricchiardone | 7th 125 cm^3 |

SQUARCIARELLI-ROCCA DI PAPA - Hillclimb
9.10.1960

| Gilberto Ricci | 4th 125 F.2 |
| Franco Arturi | 3rd 125 F.3 |

RAPALLO-MONTALLEGRO - Hillclimb
October 1960

Franco Arturi	1st 125 Sport
Battista Ricci	2nd 125 Sport
Sergio Casalini	6th 125 Sport
Gilberto Ricci	3rd 125 F.2
Aldo Cresta	6th 125 F.2

TROFEO CADETTI - Monza - Track speed event
October 1960

Luciano Spinello	8th 125 cm^3
Angelo Orsenigo	11th 125 cm^3
Gianni Polenghi	12th 125 cm^3

Silvano Forcella	15th 125 cm^3
Giovanni Varchi	16th 125 cm^3
Giuseppe Visenzi	17th 125 cm^3
Gilberto Ricci	18th 125 cm^3
Alfredo Gabba	19th 125 cm^3
Giovanni Maranesi	21st 125 cm^3
Sandro Casalini	22nd 125 cm^3

PISTA ROSSA - Milano - Go-kart speed event
1.11.1960

| Franco Moriggia | 5th Dogi Rumi |
| Gianni Zonca | 6th Dogi Rumi |

RECCO-USCIO - Hillclimb
November 1960

Battista Ricci	1st 125 Sport
Franco Arturi	2nd 125 Sport
Tonino Nesci	3rd 125 Sport
Sandro Casalini	5th 125 Sport
Lino Chembini	6th 125 Sport
Gilberto Ricci	1st 125 F.2
Giuseppe Ricci	4th 125 F.2
Aldo Cresta	5th 125 F.2
Mario Pesce	6th 125 F.2

KART RACE - Parma
13.11.1960

| Enzo Mereghetti | 3rd Dogi Rumi |
| G. Piero Gagliardi | 8th Dogi Rumi |

At the end of the 1960 season:

Gilberto Ricci riding a Rumi, took 2nd place in the F.2 125 cm^3 class of the Italian Hillclimb Championship.

Franco Arturi riding a Rumi, took 2nd place in the 125 cm^3 Sport class of the Italian Hillclimb Championship.

Luciano Spinello riding a Rumi, took 3rd place in the 125 cm^3 Sport class of the Italian Hillclimb Championship.

1961

DORIA-CRETO - Hillclimb
April 1961

Orlando Mion	2nd
Giuseppe Ricci	4th
Aldo Cresta	9th

VOLTRI-TURCHINO - Hillclimb
11.5.1961

Franco Arturi	1st 125 Sport
Gilberto Ricci	2nd 125 Sport
Elio Monti	3rd 125 Sport
Orlando Mion	2nd 125 Sport

PEGAZZANO-BIASSA - F.3 Hillclimb
14.5.1961

| Franco Arturi | 2nd 125 F.3 |
| Gilberto Ricci | 3rd 125 F.3 |

SASSI-SUPERGA - Hillclimb
2.6.1961

Franco Arturi	3rd
Elio Monti	4th
Gilberto Ricci	5th

SAVONA-CADIBONA - Hillclimb
12.6.1961

On the facing page, Aldo Mirimin, aboard a specially prepared Rumi 125, in action during a trials event held in June 1961 in the Valle Ceppi, near Turin.

254

Franco Arturi	1st 125 F.3
Elio Monti	2nd 125 F.3
Battista Renzi	3rd 125 F.3
Orlando Mion	2nd 125 F.2
Giuseppe Rizzi	6th 125 F.2

CERNOBBIO-BISBINO - Hillclimb
9.7.1961

Franco Arturi	4th 125 F.2
Giuseppe Ricci	7th 125 F.2
Giuseppe Cassani	9th 125 F.2

VINCI-SAN BERNARDO - Hillclimb
23.7.1961

| Franco Arturi | 4th 125 F.2 |

BOBBIO-PENICE - Hillclimb
23.7.1961

| Orlando Mion | 3rd 125 F.2 |

PONTEDECIMO-GIOVI - International hillclimb
15.9.1961

Orlando Mion	2nd 125 F.2
Giuseppe Ricci	5th
Gaetano Basilio	9th

OULTON PARK - Great Britain

| John Dixon | 11th 125 Gentleman |

On the facing page, the 1963 Bergrennen Maocherenz event (CH). The photo shows Roland Wangart, who came fourth aboard a Rumi "Junior" fitted with Earles forks and megaphones.

Printed by D'Auria Industrie Grafiche S.p.A
Ascoli Piceno, Italy, August 2005